CW01582841

Making Sense of Vocabulary

Christine Digby and John Myers

CASSELL

CASSELL PUBLISHERS LIMITED
Villiers House, 41/47 Strand
London WC2N 5JE

First published 1991

British Library Cataloguing in Publication Data
Digby, Christine
Making sense of vocabulary.
1. English language. Vocabulary
I. Title II. Myers, John
428.1

ISBN 0-304-33016-7

British Library Cataloguing in Publication Data
Digby, Christine
Making sense of vocabulary.-Self study ed.
1. English language. Vocabulary
I. Title II. Myers, John
428.1

ISBN 0-304-33013-2

Illustrations by Taurus Graphics, Harry Venning
Typeset by Colset Private Limited, Singapore
Printed in Great Britain by The Bath Press

Contents

Introduction

Making Sense of Vocabulary presents and practises some 1500 items of English vocabulary through a variety of topics and themes chosen to be interesting and relevant to all learners of English from Elementary level upwards.

Each of the 17 units uses example texts, illustrations, puzzles or games to give you a closer idea of the meaning and use of the new vocabulary. These are followed by enjoyable exercises designed to check your understanding of the new words.

We have also included an alphabetical word list with a guide to the pronunciation of each item which will help you to remember the words you have learnt, remind you how to say them, and refer you back to the unit they appeared in.

Christine Digby
John Myers

1 Travel and transport

BY LAND, SEA AND AIR

1 Choose your transport

Match the words below to the pictures.

a hovercraft **b** foot **c** plane **d** train **e** bus **f** bicycle
g taxi **h** coach **i** ferry **j** tube (underground)

2 How to go

When you travel using the methods of transport in Exercise 1 above, you can say:

I'm going *by* train.
by car.
by bus.

Which, in the list in Exercise 1, is the only different one?

I'm going *on* ________________________.

3 Where to catch it

You can take a bus at the *bus station*.
a plane at the *airport*.

Where can you catch these? Match the words on the left with the places on the right.

1 coach	**a** rank
2 ferry	**b** station
3 taxi	**c** port

4 What kind of journey?

Complete the sentences using the words in the box below.

a We went by plane and during the ______________ we watched a good film.

b We went by train and during the ______________ we had a good sleep.

c We went by ferry and during the ______________ we had a good meal.

d We went by bike and during the ______________ we saw some lovely views.

crossing	ride	flight	journey

TRAVELLING BY TRAIN

5 Conversation

Complete the conversations below by putting the missing letters into the words. The first one has been done for you.

At the Ticket Office

Passenger:	A ticket to Birmingham, please.	
Ticket Officer:	S_ingl_e or return?	a) ngil
Passenger:	Return, please. I'm coming back next Sunday. Can I r_________e a seat in advance? I know the train is often very full.	b) esvre
Ticket Officer:	Certainly. That's £76.90 please. Here's your ticket and your s_________t n_________r.	c) ea buem

At the station

Passenger:	Where's the Birmingham train, please?	
Porter:	On p_________m 7, sir.	d) fatorl
	Over there, next to the tourist information o_________e.	e) ficf
Passenger:	Is there a b_________t on the train where I can get something to eat?	f) fefu
Porter:	Yes.	
Passenger:	Do I have to change before Birmingham?	
Porter:	No, it's a d_________t train.	g) rcie
	Here's a t_________e with all the information you need – times of the trains, days it runs, everything.	h) tbeimla

On the train

Passenger 1:	Excuse me, madam. This is a No s__________g compartment.	i) imkon
Passenger 2:	Sorry. I didn't see the sign.	
Inspector:	T__________s, please	j) ikcet
Passenger 1:	Here you are.	
Inspector:	This is a f__________t c__________s compartment, sir, and you've only got a s__________d c__________s ticket. You must pay a £25 supplement.	k) rsi las l) aandrt las

6 The station

Label the pictures below using words from the exercises above.

c ______________ d ______________ e ______________

b ______________

a ______________

f ______________

g ______________

TRAVELLING BY PLANE

7 Signs

Match the signs to the sentences below.

a **Car park** b **Exit** c **Check in**

d **Boarding Pass : Window 12J** e **Duty free**

f **Baggage collection** g **Departure lounge**

h **Car hire** i **Trolleys** j **Immigration**

k **Customs** l **Passport control**

1 You can buy cheap wine, spirits, perfume and cigarettes in this shop. ________
2 This is a ticket which shows your seat number on the plane. ________
3 You can rent a car here. ________
4 This is where you wait for your plane. ________
5 This is where you find your luggage when you get off the plane. ________
6 This is where you show your passport when you enter a country. ________
7 This is where the officers sometimes ask you to open your suitcase. ________
8 You can leave your car here. ________
9 If you follow these signs you will find your way out of the building. ________
10 You can put your suitcases on one of these and push them round the airport. ________
11 This is where you show your passport when you leave a country. ________
12 This is where you give your luggage in before your flight. ________

8 Holiday in the UK

Imagine you are driving to the airport in New York and taking the plane from the USA to Britain, where you will rent a car. Put the signs into the order in which you would normally see them during your trip. (You may see some twice.)

1 car park
2 ______
3 ______
4 ______
5 ______
6 ______
7 ______
8 ______
9 ______
10 ______
11 ______
12 ______

TRAVELLING BY CAR

9 Word pictures

Look at these pictures. What words can you see?

a ______

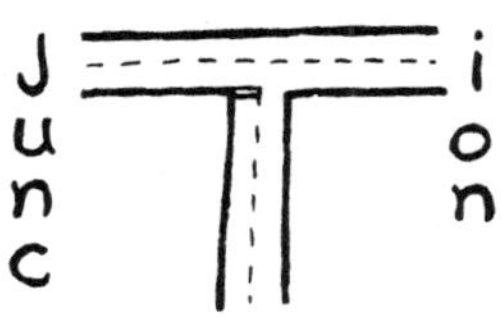

b ______

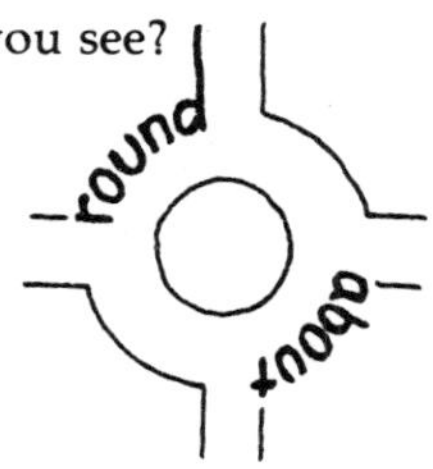

c ______

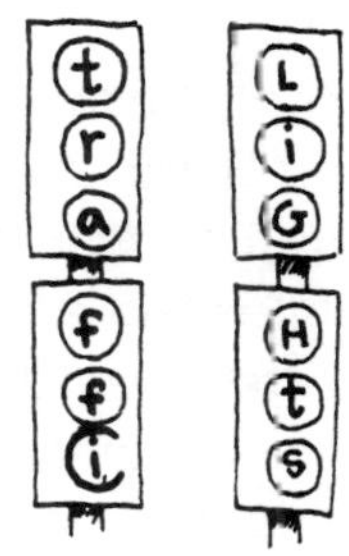

d ______

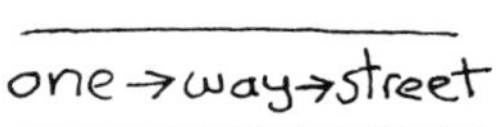

e ______

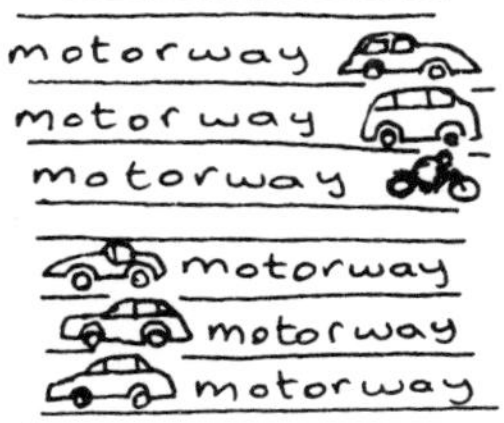

f ______

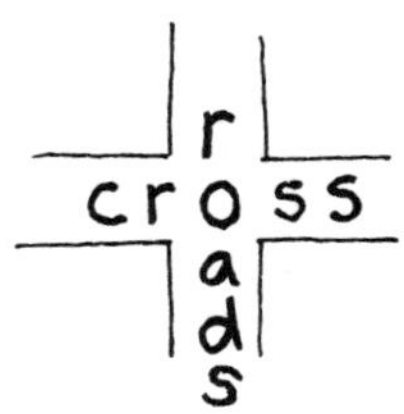

g ______

h ______

i ______

j ______

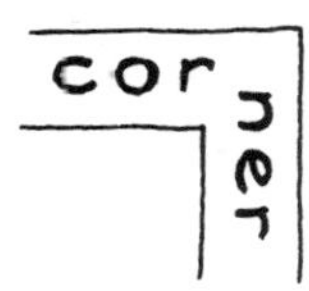

k ______

10 Street furniture

Complete the sentences below using some of the words from Exercise 9.

1 This road takes traffic round the town centre: ____________

2 You can drive fast on this road: ____________

3 This crosses a river or a railway: ____________

4 You can only drive in one direction down this street: ____________

5 You should stop if you see red: ____________

6 You can walk under a busy street through this: ____________

7 This goes under a mountain or river: ____________

8 Where roads meet, there can be a ________, a ________ or a ________.

11 Which way next?

Read the following directions and write down the place you arrive at.

Drive along the motorway and go through the tunnel under the hill south of the town. Leave the motorway before the bypass at Junction 13 and turn left at the roundabout. Drive over the bridge into town and go straight through the first set of traffic lights. After about 200 metres you'll come to a T junction. Turn right here and then left at the first set of traffic lights. Take the second right down a one-way street and it is on the corner just past the second crossroads on the left.

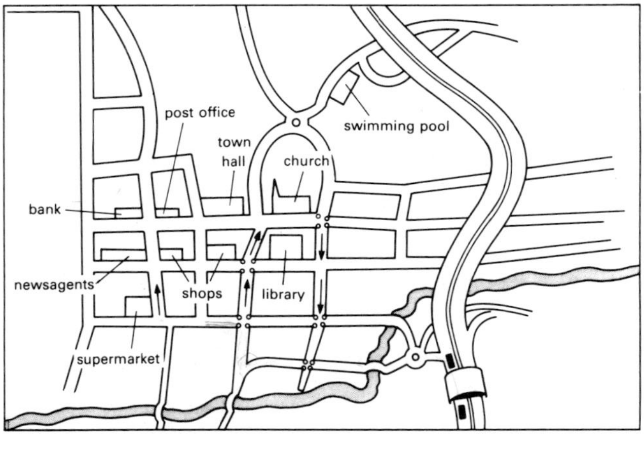

I've arrived at the ____________.

2 Work

PEOPLE, PLACES AND ADJECTIVES

1 Where do they work?

Write the names of the people in the circle next to the places where they work.

doctor waiter/waitress
sales assistant pilot
attendant mechanic
steward/stewardess
chef nurse

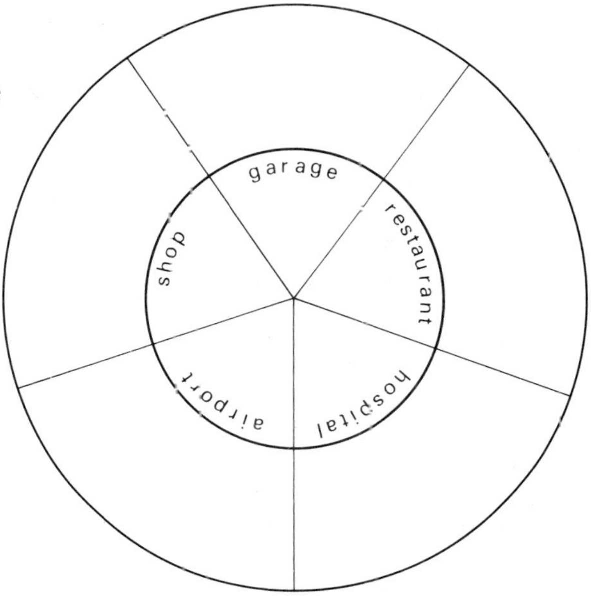

2 Who does what?

Complete the sentences below using the jobs from the list in Exercise 1.

1 The person who fills your car with petrol is called the ________________.
2 The person who flies the plane is the ________________.
3 The person who prepares the food in a restaurant is called the ________________.
4 The person who brings the food to the table is called the ________________.
5 The person who brings the food and drinks to you in the plane is called the ________________.
6 The person who repairs your car is called the ________________.

3 Describing jobs

Match the adjectives on the left with their opposites on the right. They all describe jobs.

1 part-time	5 interesting
2 temporary	6 skilled
3 well-paid	7 stressful
4 clean	

a dirty	e full-time
b boring	f relaxing/easy
c unskilled	g badly-paid
d permanent	

4 Who is talking?

Choose from the list of jobs in Exercise 1.

1 'It's a highly skilled job – I've studied for several years. It's quite stressful because you've often got a lot of people to look after. The hours are very long, and it's a badly-paid job – we earn much less than the doctors.'

2 'It's only a part-time job – I only work in the evenings. I hope it will be only a temporary one – I don't want to do this for very long – it's dirty and badly-paid. You get quite cold too standing in the rain and it's also very boring doing the same thing again and again – one car is much the same as another.'

3 'I'm unskilled and left school with very few certificates and no training. This is my first job. It's quite stressful, surprisingly – queues of people waiting with their shopping – some of them get quite angry with me. One day, though, if I stay long enough, maybe I'll get the manager's job!'

HOW TO GET A JOB

5 What comes first?

Put the following sentences into the correct order.

a	The company needs another person.	1
b	You apply for the post.	
c	You earn more money.	
d	You see the advert.	
e	You arrange an appointment for an interview.	
f	They advertise in the paper.	
g	You accept the job.	
h	You have an interview.	
i	You do well and get promotion.	
j	You retire at 60.	
k	They offer you the job.	
l	They employ you for 40 years.	

6 Complete the table

Use some of the words in Exercise 5.

	Verb	Noun
	advertise	advert/advertisement
1	____________	application
2	____________	acceptance
3	____________	arrangement
4	interview	____________
5	____________	offer
6	____________	employment
7	____________	earnings
8	promote	____________
9	____________	retirement

7 Complete the sentences

Choose one word from Exercise 6 to complete these sentences.

1 Please send me an a____________ form.

2 We e____________ more than 200 people in this factory.

3 More people nowadays take early r____________ and stop work at 50.

4 Weekly e____________ start at £200 and go up to £350.

5 You've got a good chance of p____________ – in two years you could be the manager.

BUSINESS LETTERS

8 A formal letter

Label this letter **a** to **g** from the following list.

a date **b** address of the person sending the letter **c** address of the person receiving the letter **d** initials **e** surname **f** position **g** signature

1

2

3

Dear Mr Smith

With reference to your letter of 19 June, I am writing to confirm the arrangements.

I enclose a copy of the document in question and I would be grateful if you could send me any information you have on the matter.

I look forward to your reply.

Yours sincerely

4

5 6

7

9 Business letter expressions

What do these expressions mean in everyday English? Match the 'business letter' expressions on the left with the expressions on the right.

1 *Dear Mr Smith*
2 *With reference to your letter of 19 June* I am writing to confirm the arrangements.
3 *I enclose* a copy of the document in question.
4 *I would be grateful if you could* send me any information you have on the matter.
5 *I look forward to your reply.*
6 *Yours sincerely*

a 'Please . . .'
b 'Hello'
c 'Goodbye'
d 'I'm talking about that letter you sent me . .'
e 'Hope to hear from you soon'
f 'I'm sending you. . .'

IN THE OFFICE

10 Which is right?

Circle the correct expression in brackets to match the one underlined in the sentence. Look up the alternative in a dictionary if you are not sure of its meaning.

1 I can't have a drink with you now, I'm working. (*I'm on duty/off duty*)
2 I haven't got much money at the moment because I haven't got a job. (*I'm at work/out of work*)
3 Sorry, the lift doesn't work. (*It's out of order/on order*)
4 We'll deliver it by messenger this afternoon. (*We'll send it by hand/by post*)
5 All our equipment is very modern. (*It's out of date/up to date*)
6 These shoes are cheaper this month. (*They're on sale/in the sale*)

11 Office furniture

Read the paragraph and look at the picture. Write the words underlined in the correct places below.

Debbie arrived at work late and her secretary was already busy on her typewriter. When she looked in her diary lying open on her desk she saw that she had an appointment with an important client at 11. She asked her secretary to open the morning post and reply to any letters herself. The secretary got up and went to the photocopier in the corner and then put the copies of the documents in the filing cabinet behind her desk.

Debbie started to prepare herself for the meeting. She switched on the computer on her desk and wrote down in her note pad the latest figures displayed on the VDU screen in front of her. She added the figures up on her calculator and compared them to those on the chart on the wall. Then she took out her address book from the drawer, but she couldn't find the number of the restaurant she wanted. She looked it up in the telephone directory and booked a table for two for lunch on the phone. Now she was ready for anything.

The telephone rang and the receptionist told her the client had cancelled the meeting.

1 ______________________ 8 ______________________

2 ______________________ 9 ______________________

3 ______________________ 10 ______________________

4 ______________________ 11 ______________________

5 ______________________ 12 ______________________

6 ______________________ 13 ______________________

7 ______________________ 14 ______________________

3 Home life

THE HOUSE THAT HAS EVERYTHING

1 Word puzzle

Find the rooms and parts of the house hidden in the puzzle. One has been done for you. There are 10 more.

S	T	A	I	R	S	X	P	F	A
T	S	P	A	R	E	R	O	O	M
U	Z	K	I	T	C	H	E	N	T
D	I	N	I	N	G	A	M	E	S
Y	B	A	T	H	R	B	E	D	R
Q	R	S	G	V	O	H	J	P	O
H	D	R	I	C	O	B	N	I	O
A	W	O	P	X	M	H	L	R	M
L	A	N	D	I	N	G	Y	M	K
L	I	V	I	N	G	R	O	O	M

a d ining r oom

b k itchen

c g ym

d l anding

e s tairs

f s pare r oom : bedroom kept for visitors.

g b athroom

h s tudy

i g ames r oom

j h all

k l iving r oom

2 Your house

Complete these sentences with words from the puzzle.

1 When you come in through the front door of a house the first place you often stand is the hall

2 You normally cook in the kitchen

3 You sleep in the ______

4 Some houses have a room where you eat. It's called the ______

5 In a house with more than one floor, you walk up and down the ______

6 The bedrooms and bathroom upstairs often have doors onto the ______

7 Some houses have a room where you can do exercises and keep fit. It's called the ______

8 When there is an extra room in a house, some people make this the ______ ______ where children can play.

9 Some people use the extra room to work in. It's called the ______

10 Some people have a bedroom for guests. This is called the ______

11 The room where you watch TV and relax is called the ______

12 You wash and have a shower in the ______

SOFT FURNISHINGS

3 Where do you find them?

Where do you normally find the things on the left? Choose from the places on the right.

sheets		
curtains		
carpet		
towel		door
tablecloth	on the	window
blankets	at the	chair
rug	in the	table
pillow		bathroom
blinds		bed
napkin		floor
cushion		
flannel		
placemat		

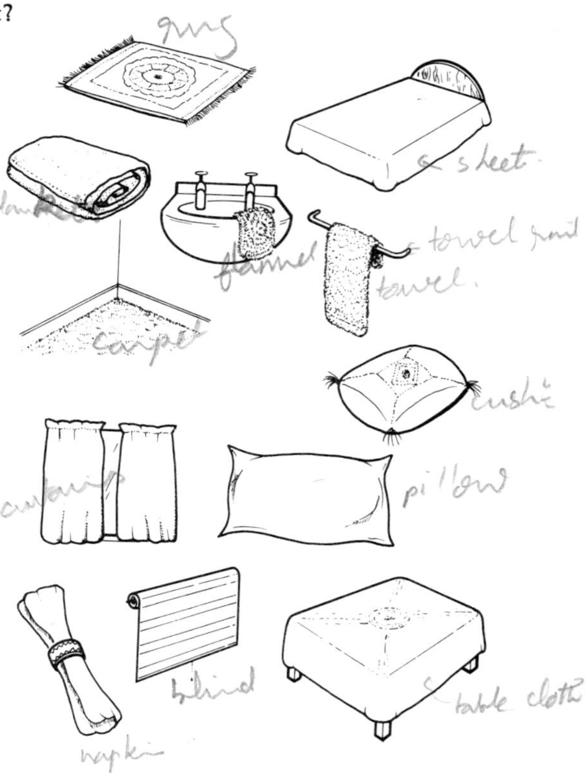

4 Similar but different

Complete the sentences by putting the correct word in the blanks.

1 **cushion/pillow**
Both can be square and filled with feathers, but you put the
a) __pillow__ under your head in bed, and the
b) __cushe__ behind you on a chair.

2 **carpet/rug**
Both are laid on the floor, but the **a)** __carpet__ goes across the room from wall to wall, and the **b)** __rug__ is much smaller.

3 **sheets/blankets**
Both can be put on the bed, but the **a)** __sheets__ are put under you and over you and are often made of cotton, and the **b)** __blankets__ are put on top to keep you warm and are often made of wool.

4 **towel/flannel**
Both can be found in the bathroom, but you use the small
a) __flannel__ to wash yourself, and the large
b) __towel__ to dry yourself after the bath or shower.

5 **curtains/blinds**
Both are used to keep out the sun and can be closed at night, but **a)** __curtains__ are made of soft material and you pull them across the window, and **b)** __blinds__ are made of plastic or hard material and you usually pull them down the window.

6 **napkin/tablecloth**
Both are found on the table, but the large **a)** __tablecloth__ covers the table, and the small **b)** __napkin__ is used to wipe your mouth and hands after the meal.

WOMAN'S WORK OR MAN'S WORK?

5 Who's the boss?

Read the first part of the conversation below and decide which is the husband – A or B.

A: Why do I always have to do all the housework? I do the cooking, the washing – your clothes and mine – the ironing, the cleaning . . . .

B: Just a minute, I often do the shopping and I always do the washing-up after the meals; and I make the bed every morning.

A: OK, but I do the polishing – all the silver, and the wooden tables and chairs.

B: But I've done all the decorating – I painted the ceilings, walls and windows.

A: And I did the tidying up after you – you made such a mess, I had to put everything away and clean up.

Now read the second part and see if you were right.

B: I'm making the shelves for the books in the living-room, and the coffee table you wanted.
A: Yes, and I'll do the dusting and hoovering when you finish.
B: Why don't you sit down and have a rest? I'll make the breakfast this morning.
A: That makes a change! That'll give me time to make a phone call to my solicitor . . . . 'Hello, this is Mr Smith . . . .'

6 *Do* and *Make*

Complete the table below. Which activities take *do*, which take *make*? Try to do it without looking at the text to see how much you can remember.

the decorating	the shopping	the washing
the washing-up	the meals	the ironing
the dusting	a mess	the polishing
the hoovering	a phone call	the tidying up
the bed	a change	

make	do
furniture	the housework

FURNITURE, FIXTURES AND APPLIANCES

7 Word pictures

What words can you see in these pictures?

a sink b armchair c cupboard d washing machine e Fridge - Freezer

f wardrobe g sofa h basin i cooker j Mirror

8 What do you use?

Answer the following questions with one of the words from the list in Exercise 7.

1 You want to find a plate or glass. Where do you look? In the cupboard.
2 You want to find your suit. Where do you look? In the wardrobe
3 You want to sit close to someone. Where do you sit? On the sofa
4 You want to sit comfortably and read a book. Where do you sit? On the armchair
5 You want to wash your hands. Where do you do it? in the basin
6 You want to wash your knife and fork. Where do you do it? in the sink.
7 You want to keep something cold. Where do you put it? in the fridge
8 You want to keep something very cold for a long time. Where do you put it?
in the freezer.
9 You wash plates, glasses etc automatically in a dishwasher, where do you wash clothes? in a washing machine.
10 The person who prepares the meal is the cook. What machine does he or she cook on? On the cooker.

4 People

FAMILIES

1 Family Tree

Using the information in the diagram and the words below, complete the letter to a penfriend.

m = married

cousins	brother	brother-in-law	husband	wife
mother	aunt	grandparents	children	nephew
sister	niece	uncle		

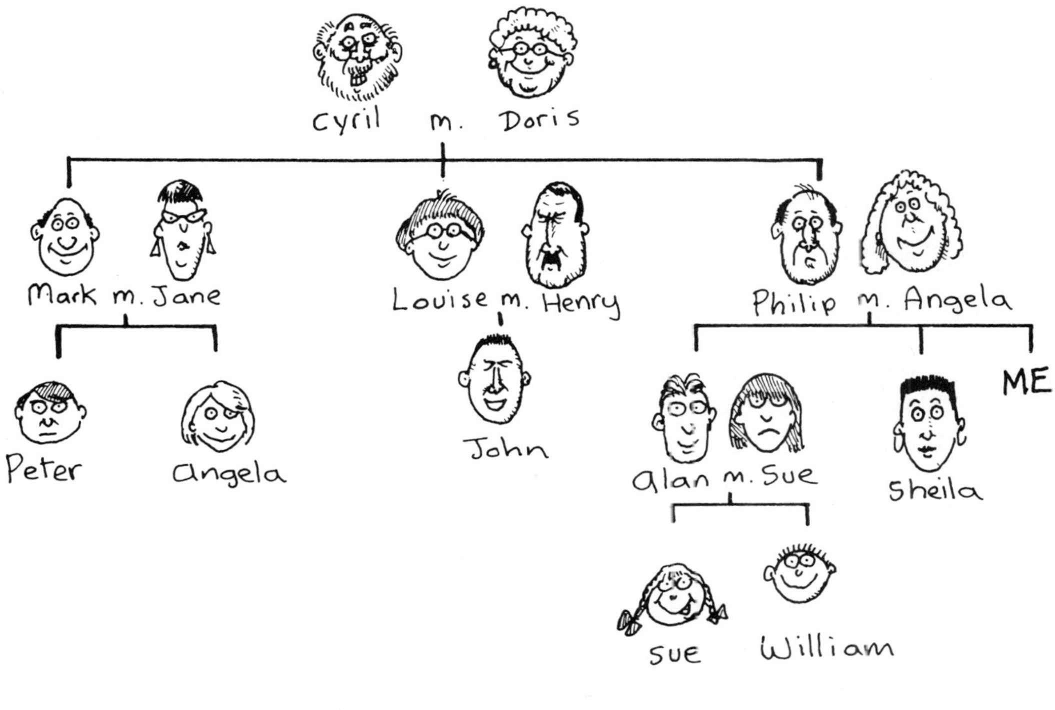

Dear Theresa

Thank you for your letter. I feel I know you better now that you've told me more about yourself and your family.

I'll tell you a little about my family. I'm the youngest of a family of three children. Alan my a)_____ is the oldest. He's married and they've got two b)______. My three-year old c)______ is called Sue, the same name as her d)______ and my e)______, William, is just two. Then there's my f)______, Sheila. She's getting married next July. I'm looking forward to it because my future g)______ lives in Jamaica and they're going to go there to live, so I expect I'll be able to visit them. I've got three h)______, Peter, Angela and John.

My i)______, Mark is my father's brother, but we don't often see him. I don't know what the problem is, but I know his j)______, Jane, never talks to my parents. My father gets on much better with my k)______, Louise and her l)______, Henry. My m)_______ are quite old now. They've got very old-fashioned names – Cyril and Doris. You rarely hear names like that these days.

Looking forward to hearing from you soon

[illegible]

WHAT IS HE/SHE LIKE?

2 Adjectives

Choose the correct adjective to complete these sentences.

1 **friendly/unfriendly**
The people I met there were very ____________ – they talked to me in the street, bought me drinks and even invited me into their homes for dinner.

2 **enthusiastic/unenthusiastic**
He's not interested in anything. He just wants to sit at home and watch TV. He's ____________ about anything new I suggest.

3 **confident/unconfident**
She's very shy and ____________ – she doesn't like meeting new people and she's very unsure of herself.

4 **kind/unkind**
My neighbour is extremely ____________. When I was ill she visited me every day, she did my shopping, cooked my meals and even cleaned the house for me.

5 **selfish/unselfish**
They are such ____________ people – they never think about themselves, they always think of other people first.

6 **reliable/unreliable**
He is so ____________ – he never arrives on time and he often forgets to do what you asked him to.

7 **honest/dishonest**
Don't lend him any money – he's very ____________ and you may never see it again.

8 **patient/impatient**
I'm sorry I'm late. Thank you for being so ____________ and not getting angry with me.

3 Qualities

Using the adjectives in Exercise 2, what *two* qualities do you think are most important for the following people to have or not to have?

a I think a teacher should be ______________________________

b I think a husband/wife should be ______________________________

c I think a dog should be ______________________________

d I don't think a policeman should be ______________________________

e I don't think an assistant in the office should be ______________________________

THE FIVE AGES OF MAN

4 The times of your life

Look at this scale.

older ↑	pensioner	60/65
	adult	18+
	teenager	13–19
	child	3–12
younger ↓	baby	0–2

Now use the words to complete the sentences below.

1 Ten years ago he was an angry ____________. Now at 27 he is a world-famous tennis star.
2 Young people under 18 must be accompanied by an ____________.
3 After a long life you can enjoy some of the good things about being a ____________ like cheaper travel.
4 The ____________ was born at 2 o'clock and weighed 4 kilos.
5 I lived in Australia when I was a ____________ and moved to the States when I was 11.

5 Similar but different

These adjectives are similar in meaning, but one is more positive (+) and the other is more negative (–). Complete the sentences below.

1 childlike (+)/childish (–)
- a He is quite an old man, but he still has a ____________ enthusiasm for new ideas and inventions.
- b He is quite an old man, but he behaves in a very ____________ way – he always expects other people to do what he wants and is angry when they don't.

2 mature (+)/middle-aged (–)
- a I don't feel young any more, I feel ____________.
- b We are looking for a ____________ woman to manage the office.

3 youthful (+)/immature (–)
- a Because he was so young, they said he was too ____________ to take difficult decisions.
- b She was nearly 70, but she still looked ____________ and healthy.

4 elderly (+)/old (–)
- a The ____________ people who come here have some interesting stories to tell.
- b You'll be sorry you smoke so much when you're ____________.

HAIR

6 Word puzzle

Find the words in the puzzle used to describe hair. There are 14 adjectives.

B	R	O	W	N	C	M	P	L
L	E	X	D	C	F	Z	Q	K
A	D	N	A	W	A	E	S	D
C	S	T	R	A	I	G	H	T
K	V	H	K	V	R	R	O	L
T	H	I	N	Y	W	E	R	O
M	A	C	U	R	L	Y	T	N
W	U	K	B	L	O	N	D	G

7 Categories

Put the words you have found into these categories.

Length s____________
l____________

Quantity t____________
t____________

Style s____________
c____________
w____________

Colour d____________
f____________
b____________
b____________
b____________
r____________
g____________

8 Hairstyles

Describe these people's hairstyles. Note the order if you have more than one adjective: **1** length **2** quantity **3** colour **4** style. Use the adjectives from Exercise 6.

1

2

3

4

5

Example

He's got short wavy hair and a long thick moustache.

1 ______________________________

2 ______________________________

3 ______________________________

4 ______________________________

5 ______________________________

5 Food and drink

EATING IN

1 Things you need

Label the kitchen utensils and the parts of the cooker using the words below.

kettle saucepan frying pan oven grill hot plate

toaster microwave liquidizer percolator

1 ____________	6 ____________
2 ____________	7 ____________
3 ____________	8 ____________
4 ____________	9 ____________
5 ____________	10 ____________

2 Ways of cooking

Complete the sentences using **a**) the verbs from the list below and **b**) the words you have learnt in Exercise 1. (Some may be used more than once.)

a) verbs: **grill** **fry** **roast** **bake** **steam** **boil**

1 To make boiled eggs, you **a**) ____________ the eggs in water in a **b**) ____________ on the **b**) ____________ for about three minutes.

2 If you want potato soup, put the boiled potatoes into the **b)** ______________ for a couple of minutes with a little milk and butter and then heat.

3 To make fried eggs, you **a)** fry______________ the eggs in oil in a **b)** frying pan on the **b)** hotplate______________ for about 2 minutes.

4 To make steamed rice, you **a)** ______________ the rice over some water in a **b)** ______________ on the **b)** ______________ for about thirty minutes.

5 To make toast, you **a)** toast______________ the bread under the **b)** toaster______________ for about a minute and then turn it over and do the other side.

6 If you have a **b)** microwave______________ you can make toast much more quickly.

7 To make roast lamb, you **a)** roast______________ the meat with some oil in the **b)** oven______________ for about an hour.

8 To **a)** bake______________ a cake, you put the mixture in the **b)** oven______________ for about 40 minutes.

9 If you have a **b)** microwave______________ cooking can take minutes, not hours.

10 To make fresh coffee, you **a)** boil______________ some water in a **b)** keltte______________ and use a filter or a **b)** percolator

EATING OUT

3 Where can you go?

Find the missing word by completing the words given.

	c								
	a						s		
	f			c	p		t		
r	é	s	t	a	u	r	a	n	t
		e		n	b		n		a
		l		t			d		k
		f		e					e
				e					
		s		n					a
		e							w
		r							a
		v							y
		i							
		c							
		e							

4 Complete the sentences

Complete the sentences using the words from Exercise 3.

1 Most people go to a café just to drink, but you can find good food there nowadays.

2 A lot of large department stores have a self service where there are no waiters or waitresses. Customers collect their food from a counter and pay at the cash desk.

3 Big organisations or factories offer their workers cheap meals in the canteen.

4 You can buy hot dogs or sandwiches from a take away on the street.

5 You can sit down to a snack or a cheap meal in a stand.

6 The food and service in a restaurant is usually of a higher standard.

7 You order your food in the stand and eat it on the street or back at home.

5 From all corners of the world

In what nationality restaurant do you find these dishes?

1 pasta	a Chinese
2 hamburger	b Indian
3 stir fry	c Japanese
4 raw fish	d Italian
5 curry	e American

DESCRIBING FOOD

6 Opposites

Find the opposites by following the lines.

fresh tender ripe spicy sweet raw slimming

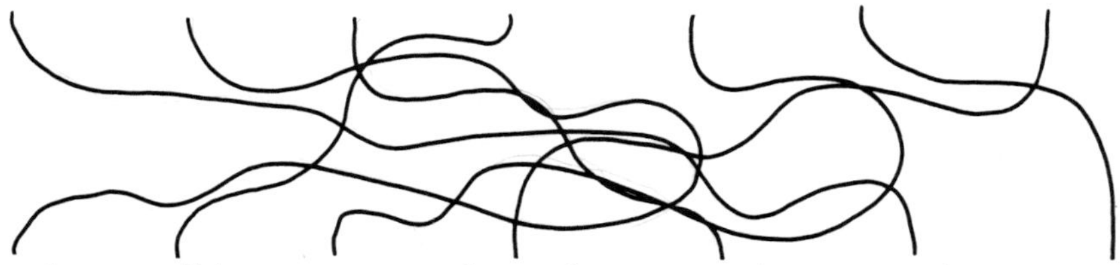

tough mild sour fattening unripe stale cooked

raw ≠ cooked
slimming ≠ fattening
fresh ≠ stale

7 Fit them in

Complete the sentences using some of the adjectives from Exericse 6.

1 I can't eat this tomato, it's green and not very ripe.
2 Could you put some sugar in this lemon juice, it's too sour.
3 This meat is almost raw, please take it back and cook it correctly.
4 I think this bread is several days old, it's so stale I can't cut it.
5 I'm on a diet, so I mustn't eat cake or sweets – they're too fattening.
6 This chicken is so tough I can't cut it.
7 The curry burnt my mouth, it was so spicy.

8 Which goes with which?

Which adjectives can be used to describe which food? Some food may be used more than once.

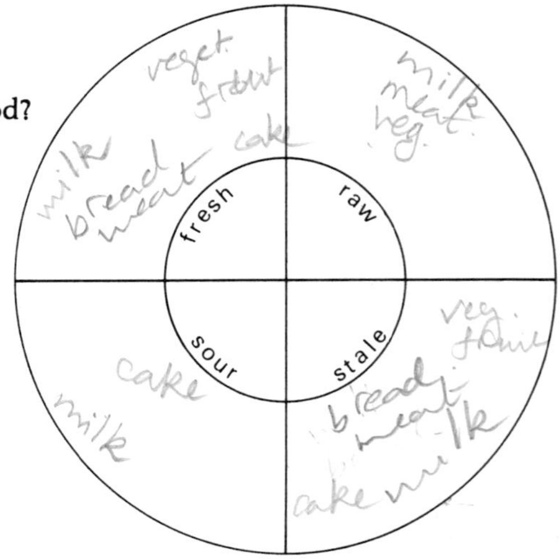

milk bread meat fish

vegetables fruit cake

DRINK

9 Alcohol

Find the drinks.

1 siykhw ______________
2 dovak ______________
3 cdrie ______________
4 eber ______________
5 ewni ______________

10 How would you like it?

Match the expressions below with the pictures.

1 on the rocks
2 neat
3 and tonic
4 with lemon
5 black
6 white
7 with cream

a

4

b
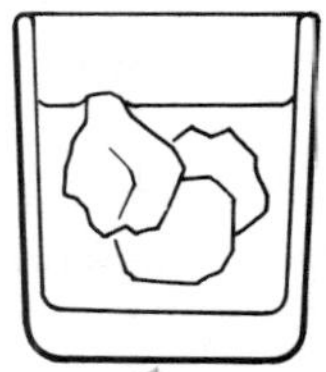
1

c

2

d

7

e

6

f

3

g

5

11 Drinks

What drinks are these people talking about? Complete the conversations below using the expressions in Exercise **10**.

1 'Your whisky, Mike. Would you like it neat or on the rocks?'
'With ice, please.'

2 'I'm afraid we haven't got any milk, would you like tea with lemon?'
'Oh, yes, that's fine.'

3 'Would you like your hot chocolate ______________?'
'No, thanks, I'm on a diet. Just with milk, please.'

4 'Do you take your coffee ______________ or ______________?'
'Just ______________ with one sugar, please.'

5 'Gin ______________?'
'Yes. With ice and a slice too, please.'

12 English tea

How to drink tea with the best. Complete the paragraph using the verbs below.

add sip boil pour stir fill

a) ______________ the water in a kettle and put the tea leaves into the warmed pot. **b)** ______________ the teapot with the hot water and leave for a few minutes. **c)** ______________ a little milk into the cup before the tea. **d)** ______________ a spoonful of sugar and **e)** ______________ gently with the silver spoon. Hold the cup delicately with the thumb and forefinger and **f)** ______________ politely and silently.

6 Sport

WHAT ARE THEY DOING?

1 The games people play

Match the pictures to the words underneath.

a

b

c

football team ____ tennis players ____ basketball side ____

2 Practising

Read the passage and find the verbs that match the pictures below.

Whatever sport you play it is important that you practise it regularly and often. If you are a footballer you can practise how to kick a ball with either foot against a goal painted on a wall. If you are a tennis player you can try to hit the ball a hundred times without stopping. Basketball players can throw the ball to each other and improve their catching.

a

b

c

d

kick ____ catch ____ hit ____ throw ____

PEOPLE IN SPORT

3 Training

Read this passage.

Both professionals and amateurs have to train for hours and hours, every day. A training programme includes many different types of physical exercises for the different parts of the body. Sometimes the exercises seem strange. For example a swimmer runs a lot to be fit.

If you train hard and exercise correctly you will begin to improve. Then you will beat opponents better than you! And you will win that match you expected to lose.

Now fill in the gaps below using words from the passage.

1 After the exercise he did special leg ______________ to regain his strength.
2 He ran the fastest time in the world and ______________ the world champion.
3 He ______________ for the Marathon race for two years by running short distances and then going for longer and longer runs.
4 The North ______________ the match against the South by 2 – 1.
5 He ______________ his first professional game but later became the most successful player in the game's history.

4 More sports

Match the pictures to the words below.

a

b

c

d

e

f

g

h

i

boxing _____ golf _____ ice-skating _____
horse-riding _____ running _____ gymnastics _____
cycling _____ racing driving _____ dancing _____

PEOPLE AND PLACES IN SPORT

5 Who plays what?

Look at this example.

Someone who runs is called a runn<u>er</u>.

Can you do the same for the other sports in Exercise 4? Be careful!
There are *two* that are different.

1 ____________________ 6 ____________________
2 ____________________ 7 ____________________
3 ____________________ 8 ____________________
4 ____________________ 9 ____________________
5 ____________________

6 Places, equipment and clothes

Draw a line to join the sports on the left with the places on the right.

boxing	course
football	court
tennis	pitch
swimming	court
golf	pool
race	ring
cricket	court
squash	course
basketball	pitch

7 What do you need?

Match the equipment and clothes shown in the pictures.

a

b

c

d

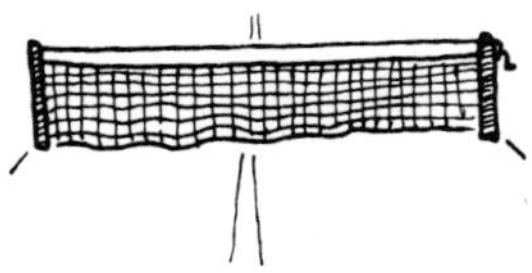

e

f

g

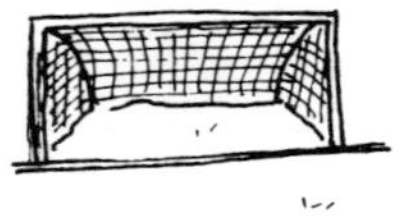

h

swimsuit _____ racket _____ glove _____ kit _____

club _____ ball _____ net _____ goal _____

GO OR PLAY?

8 Which verb?

Which verb is used with these activities and sports, *go* or *play*?

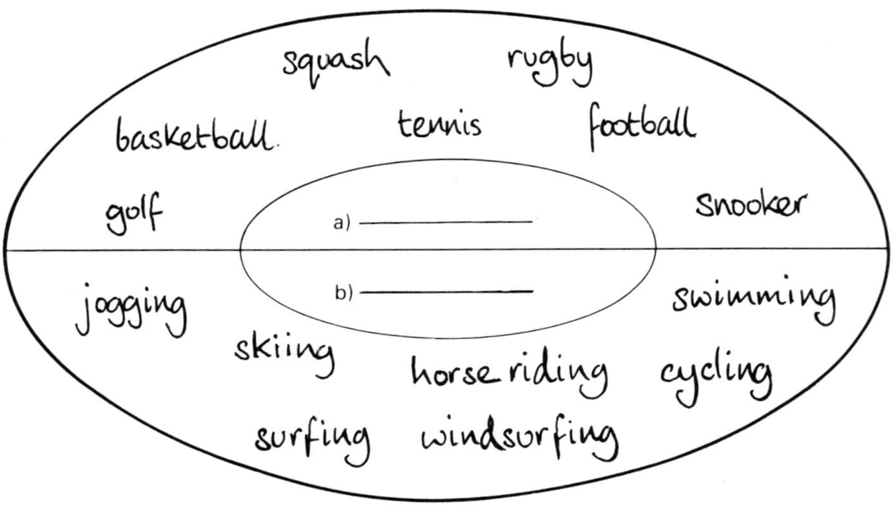

9 Word pictures

Using the pictures to help you, complete the sentences below.

1 At half time the ______________ called the rest of the team together and told them they must play better.
2 Gary Lineker scored a ______________ from 30 metres.
3 Ann Jackson and Sue Montgomery are playing against Barbara Wilson and Julie Stewart in the final of the women's ______________ competition at Wimbledon on Saturday.
4 The ______________ begins at 3.30 and all runners must be ready at the starting line by 3.25.
5 Every country wants to compete in the ______________ which are held every four years.
6 The winner receives a gold ______________, the second a silver ______________ and the third a bronze one.
7 The ______________ jumped out of their seats every time Gullit touched the ball.
8 The referee blew his ______________ to stop the match.
9 Tottenham have won the FA ______________ again by beating Arsenal 5–0 in the Final.
10 Crispin Scott has broken the world ______________ for the long jump by 18cm.

7 Health

PARTS OF THE BODY

1 Name the parts

Find the words labelled in the picture.

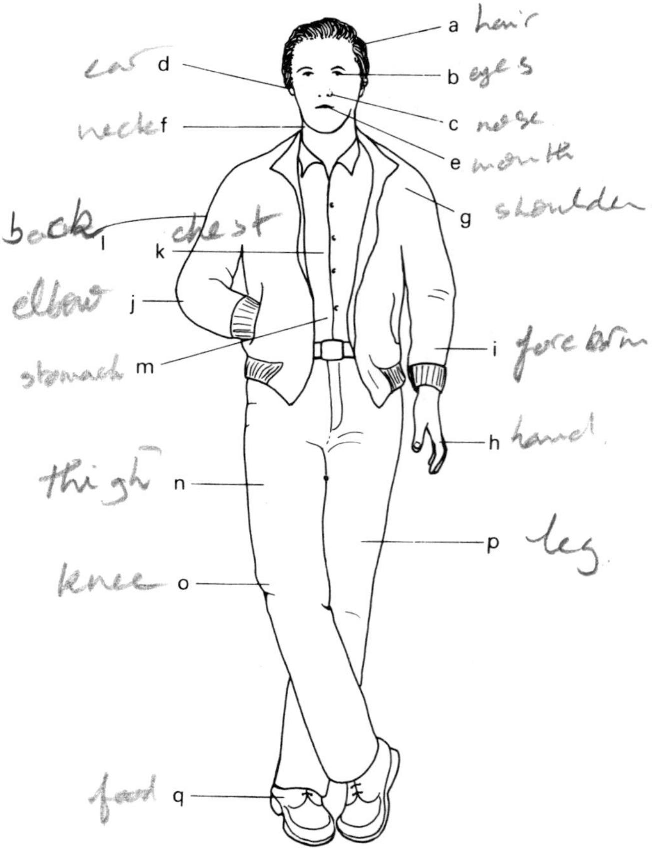

- **a** deha ____
- **b** seey ____
- **c** sneo ____
- **d** era ____
- **e** hmtuo ____
- **f** cnek ____
- **g** dsruloeh ____
- **h** nhda ____
- **i** rma ____
- **j** lbewo ____
- **k** ctseh ____
- **l** ckab ____
- **m** moatcsh ____
- **n** hitgh ____
- **o** ekne ____
- **p** gle ____
- **q** ofot ____

2 Hand or foot?

Label the pictures using the words below.

a ______________________

b ______________________

c ______________________

d ______________________

e ______________________

f ______________________

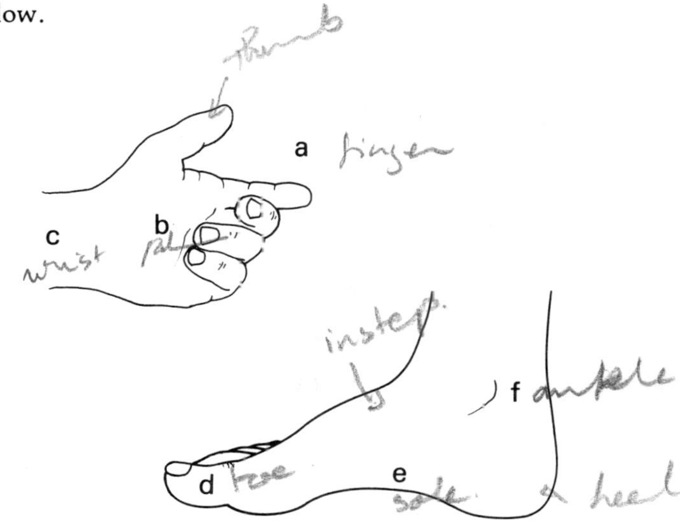

finger	ankle	toe	palm	wrist	sole

3 Where is it?

In which part of the body do you find these?

tongue

brain

heart

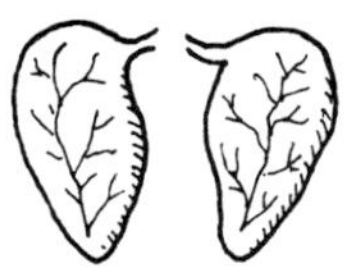

lungs

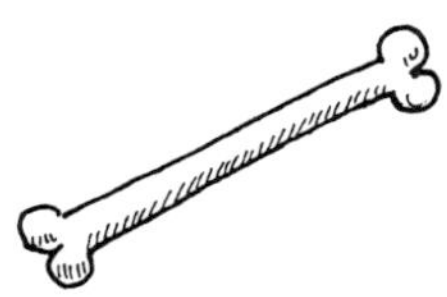

thigh bone

tooth

Example
The tongue is in the mouth.

1 The brain is in the skull.

2 The heart is in the chest.

3 The lungs are in the chest.

4 The thigh bone is in the leg.

5 A tooth is in the mouth.

ILLNESS AND INJURY

4 It hurts!

Look back at Exercise 1. What can go wrong? Label the pi:tures below.

I've got 1 a head ache.
2 a stomach-ache
3 backache.
4 toothache.

1 

2 

3 

4 

5 

6 

I've got a broken 5 my arm.
6 my nose.
7 my leg.

7 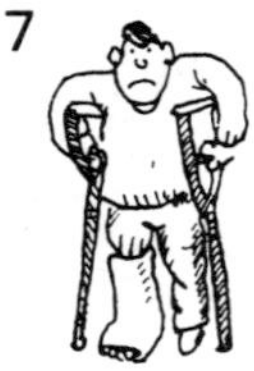

8 

9 

My 8 finger hurts.
My 9 elbow aches.

5 Health problems

Complete these sentences with some of the problems in Exercise 4.

1 A secretary who types a lot in an uncomfortable chair often has backache at the end of the day.
2 When you looked at him you could see he was a boxer because of his broken. nose
3 He ate something which was not fresh and now he's got terrible stomach-ache.
4 He came back from his skiing holiday with a pair of crutches and a broken leg

5 Please excuse my handwriting – I'm writing with my left hand because I've got a broken arm
6 Ice cream and hot drinks give me terrible toothache. I must go to the dentist.
7 I missed the nail and hit my hand with the hammer. My finger hurts.
8 The music in the disco was so loud she came home with a terrible headache.

GETTING BETTER

6 At the doctor's

Complete the dialogue with the words given in the pictures below.

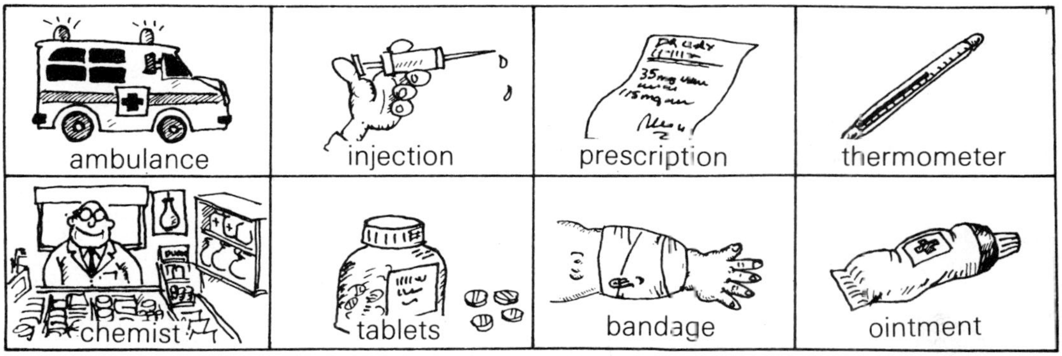

Doctor:	How are you, Mr Jones?
Patient:	I don't feel at all well, doctor. I feel ill.
Doctor:	What's the matter? Have you got a temperature?
Patient:	I'm not sure, I haven't got a **a)** thermometer at home, but I'm sure it's higher than 37°. I've taken some **b)** tablets but it's still the same.
Doctor:	I see. Anything else?
Patient:	Well, my arm is very painful. It aches when I move it. I think I need some **c)** ointment to put on it.
Doctor:	If you need anything, I'll write a **d)** prescripti for you and you can take it to the **e)** chemist. Let me see your arm. Can you take off the **f)** bandage please.
Patient:	It hurts here, doctor.
Doctor:	Have you had an **g)** injecti recently?
Patient:	Yes, doctor. We're going to Africa next week and I had a yellow fever vaccination.
Doctor:	I don't think we need to call the **h)** ambulance – it's not an emergency! In fact it's not serious at all. It's just the vaccination. Just be patient and you'll feel better in a couple of days.

7 Complete the sentences

Read Exercise 6 again and find the words or expressions to complete the sentences below.

1 The person who visits the doctor is the patient
2 If someone looks ill or unhappy, you can ask, a doctor?
3 In an emergency you must call an ambulance.
4 A vaccinati can prevent some serious diseases.
5 It's 39°C – you've got a temperature

SOUND ADVICE

8 Which word?

Circle the correct word.

1 You must give **up** / **off** smoking, Mr Fag.

2 Why don't you take **down** / **up** a new sport instead of watching it on TV all day?

3 Why don't you come in for a check **up** / **in**? We can look at your blood pressure and your weight then.

4 You can't do **with** / **without** protein – you'll starve.

5 You should cut **up** / **down** the number of sweets and chocolates you eat.

6 Parents aren't always the best people to look **at** / **after** their children.

7 If you work too hard and and don't get enough rest, you'll break **down** / **out** completely.

8 He passed **in** / **out** when he saw the blood.

9 Who takes care of what?

Label the picture and complete the sentences.

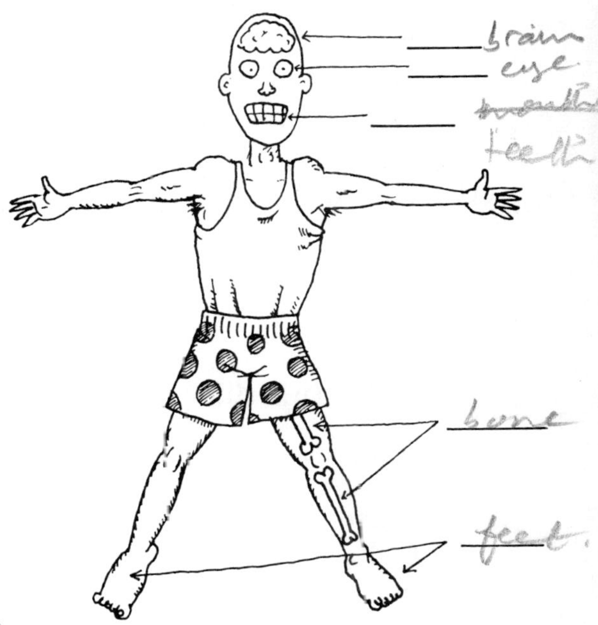

1 A surgeon takes care of your ______________.

2 A chiropodist takes care of your ______________.

3 A psychiatrist takes care of your ______________.

4 An optician takes care of your ______________.

5 A dentist takes care of your ______________.

8 Geography

HOW MUCH DO YOU KNOW?

1 Quiz

Do you know the correct answer?

1 Which is the largest ocean?
a) the Atlantic b) the Pacific c) the Indian

2 Which is the highest lake which ships can sail on?
a) Superior b) Geneva c) Titicaca

3 Which is the longest river?
a) the Nile b) the Amazon c) the Mississippi

4 Which is the longest canal?
a) the Panama b) the Corinth c) the Suez

5 Which is the highest mountain?
a) the Matterhorn b) the Eiger c) Everest

6 Which is the largest desert?
a) the Gobi b) the Sahara c) the Kalahari

7 Where is the largest rainforest?
a) in Brazil b) in Northern Australia c) in Malaysia

8 Which is the highest capital city?
a) Mexico City b) Kathmandu c) La Paz

2 Similar but different

Complete the sentences below using the correct word for each space.

1 **ocean / sea**
Both are large areas of water, but **a)** ______________ is bigger than **b)** ______________

2 **sea / lake**
Both are areas of water, but a **a)** ______________ has fresh water, and a **b)** ______________ has salt water.

3 **river / stream**
Both carry water down from higher ground, but a **a)** ______________ is smaller, narrower and has less water than a **b)** ______________

4 river / canal
Both are channels of water between two banks, but a **a)** ____________ is man-made, a **b)** ____________ is natural.

5 mountain / hill
Both are high ground, but a **a)** ____________ is not as high as a **b)** ____________.

6 forest / wood
Both are areas of trees, but a **a)** ____________ does not have as many trees as a **b)** ____________

7 city / town
Both are collections of houses and buildings, but a **a)** ____________ is larger than a **b)** ____________

8 capital city / city
Both are usually large towns, but a **a)** ____________ is the centre of government for the country and a **b)** ____________ is not.

ENGLISH IS SPOKEN HERE

3 Nationalities

Complete the table below for these English speaking countries.

Country	Nationality
He/She comes from	He/She is
the USA	American
1 ____________	English
2 ____________	Scottish
3 Ireland	____________
4 ____________	Welsh
5 Canada	____________
6 ____________	Australian
7 ____________	West Indian
8 India	____________

4 Where do they speak English?

Match the letters on the map with the countries where English is spoken.

1 England h
2 Northern Ireland ____
3 Scotland ____
4 Wales ____
5 the Republic of Ireland ____
6 the United States of America ____
7 Canada ____
8 some of the Caribbean islands ____
9 Malta ____
10 New Zealand ____
11 Nigeria ____
12 Kenya ____
13 Zimbabwe ____
14 Australia ____
15 India ____

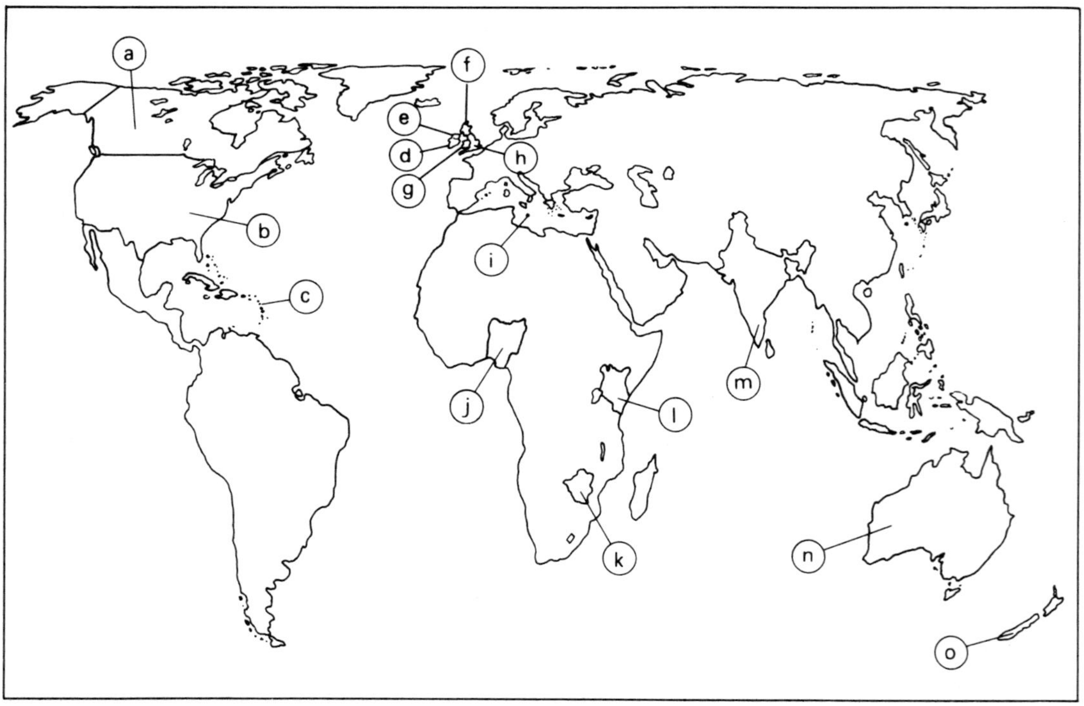

5 Languages

Now complete this table for non-English speaking countries.

Country	Nationality	Language
1 ______	French	______
2 ______	German	______
3 ______	______	Greek
4 ______	Dutch	______
5 Portugal	______	______
6 ______	Turkish	______
7 ______	______	Farsi
8 Saudi Arabia	______	______
9 Peru	______	______
10 Brazil	______	______
11 ______	Mexican	______
12 ______	______	Chinese
13 ______	Japanese	______

ROUND THE WORLD

6 Times of the day

Match the words in the box to the pictures.

midday	midnight	dawn	dusk

b ______

d ______

a ______

c ______

7 Suns, stars and planets

Complete the sentences using these words.

Pole **Moon** **stars** **hemisphere** **Equator**

Earth **Sun** **planets**

1 The ______________ goes round the ______________ every 365 days.
2 Every month we can see a new ______________
3 There are 9 ______________ in our solar system.
4 There are millions of ______________ in the galaxy.
5 On the ______________ the sun rises at 6 am and sets at 6 pm every day all year round.
6 At the North ______________ there are days when the sun never rises.
7 In the southern ______________ it's hotter in December than August.

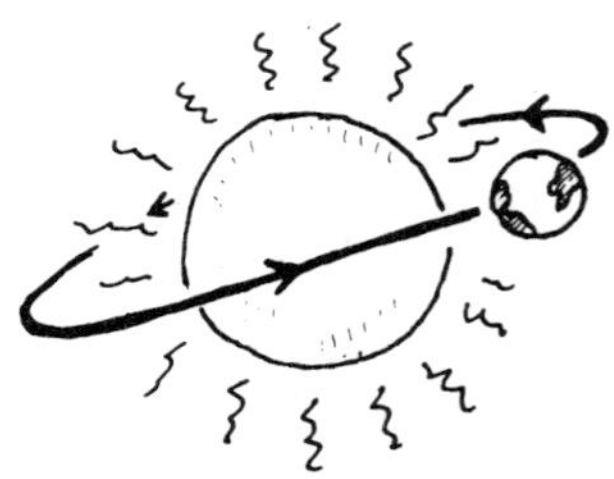

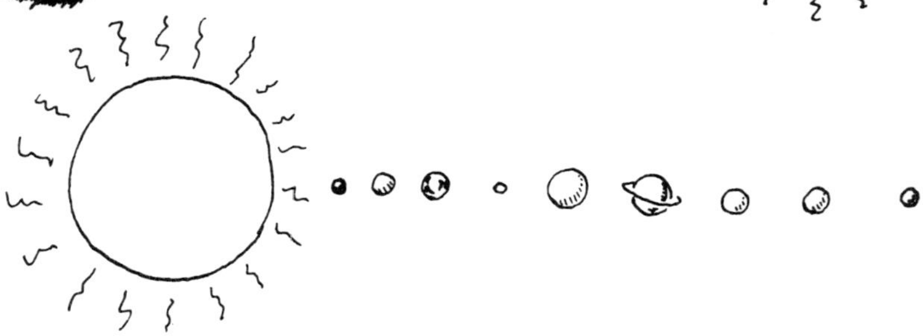

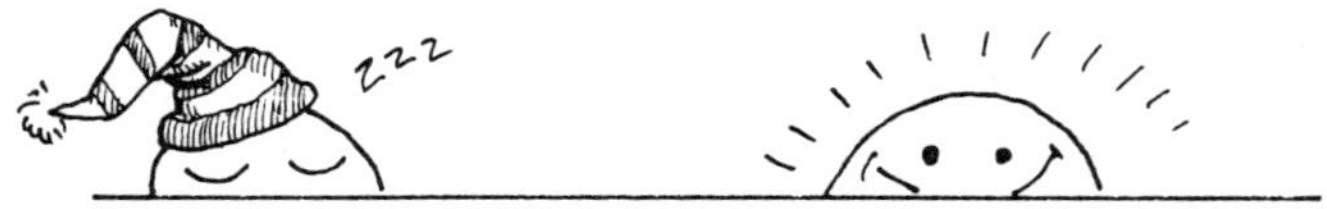

NATURAL DISASTERS

8 Word pictures

Complete the sentences below using one of the words from the pictures.

1 It rained very heavily for weeks and the river overflowed. The ______________ caused a lot of damage to fields and houses nearby.

2 The mountain was quiet for many years and people almost forgot that it was a ______________ until it erupted suddenly one day and destroyed the trees and houses on its slopes.

3 The ______________ of 1989 damaged buildings in San Francisco and many people died in their cars when a motorway collapsed.

4 Trees fell down and houses lost their roofs in the ______________ which swept up the coast of the United States.

5 There was a loud noise and suddenly the snow on the mountain came crashing down in a huge ______________ burying the village at the bottom of the valley.

6 There was no rain for two years and the ______________ meant that the farmers could not water their crops and many people died of starvation.

7 No one knew how the ______________ started but the wind pushed the flames quickly towards the town and the firemen found it difficult to put it out.

8 The boat was caught in the ______________ and was sucked down to the bottom of the sea.

9 The climate

MONTHS AND SEASONS

1 Months

Write in the missing months.

a ______________ MAY
____

b ______________ AUGUST
____

c ______________ NOVEMBER
____

d ______________ FEBRUARY
____

2 Seasons

Now write the names of the seasons under the correct pictures in Exercise 1.

spring summer autumn winter

3 Poem

There is an old poem which reminds you how many days are in each month. Can you complete it?

30 days hath S__________,
A__________, J__________ and N__________.
All the rest have __________
Excepting F__________ alone
Which has __________ days clear
And __________ days each leap year.

WHAT'S THE WEATHER LIKE?

4 Conversation

Complete the conversation below.

A: It's often very **sunny** in my country.
B: We have a lot of **sunshine** in my country, too.

A: In the winter it's quite **icy**.
B: We have a lot of **1)** ____________, too.

A: And it's **snowy** at that time, too.
B: We also have a lot of **2)** ____________.

A: In the morning, it's **3)** ____________ and cold.
B: Yes, we have a lot of **frost**, too.

A: In the autumn it's often **rainy**.
B: We often have a lot of **4)** ____________, too.

A: And sometimes it's very **5)** ____________.
B: We get some very strong **winds**.

A: In the morning it's sometimes **misty**.
B: Oh, we see some **6)** ____________, too, at that time of year.

A: But it isn't often **foggy**.
B: No, we don't have much **7)** ____________, either.

A: Today, it's just **8)** ____________
B: Yes, I think there are probably a lot of grey **clouds** in my country, too

5 Hot or cold?

Put these adjectives in the correct position on the line starting with the coldest.

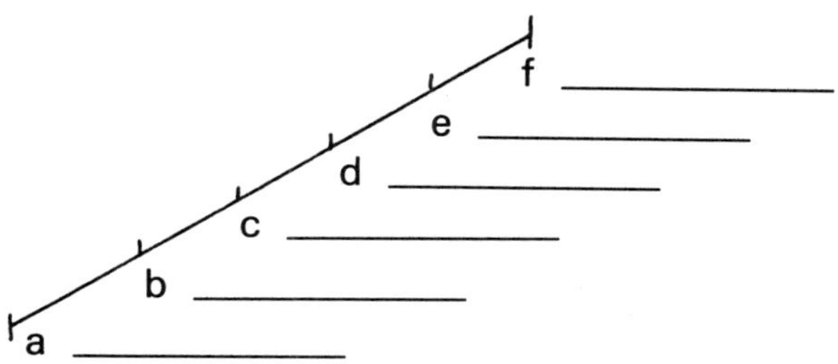

cold	warm	hot	cool	freezing	boiling

6 When do you use these?

a

b

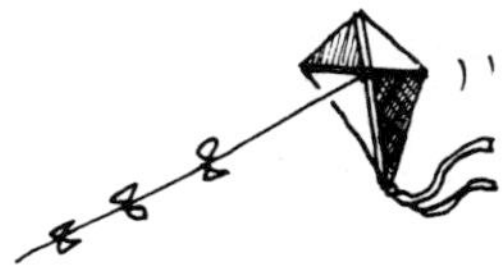

c

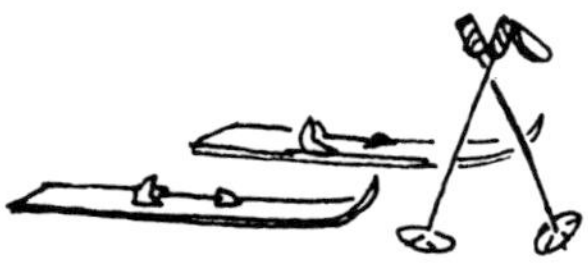

d

e

f

a When it's ______________________

b When it's ______________________

c When it's ______________________

d When it's ______________________

e When it's ______________________

f When it's ______________________

MORE WEATHER

7 Verbs

Complete the passage below using one of the verbs for each space.

rises	drops	falls	melts	freezes	blows
clear	shines				

When the wind **1)** ____________ from the east, rain often **2)** ____________ during the day. At night the temperature **3)** ____________ and the water **4)** ____________. In the morning when the clouds **5)** ____________ and the sun **6)** ____________ the temperature **7)** ____________ and the ice **8)** ____________.

8 Match them!

Match the adjectives on the left with the nouns on the right.

1 thick	a) breeze
2 strong	b) sea
3 clear	c) rain
4 rough	d) humidity
5 high	e) sky
6 heavy	f) fog
7 light	g) wind

9 Paragraphs

Using the words and expressions you have learnt, complete the paragraphs describing these 4 pictures.

a

b

c

d

1 During a hurricane the **a)** ______________ drops. There is a very **b)** ______________ wind and **c)** ______________ rain, and the sea is **d)** ______________.

2 During the day in a desert the sky is **a)** ______________ and it is hot and **b)** ______________. But at night it is very **c)** ______________ and you need to wear warm clothes.

3 In a tropical rainforest it is hot and the **a)** ______________ is high. There is often **b)** ______________ **c)** ______________, sometimes as much as 5 cms a day.

4 On top of Mount Everest it is **a)** ______________ with snow and **b)** ______________ which never **c)** ______________ and strong **d)** ______________ which **e)** ______________ the clouds across the peak.

THE WEATHER FORECAST

10 Using the map to help you, draw the symbols on page 53 next to the expressions used by the weather forecaster.

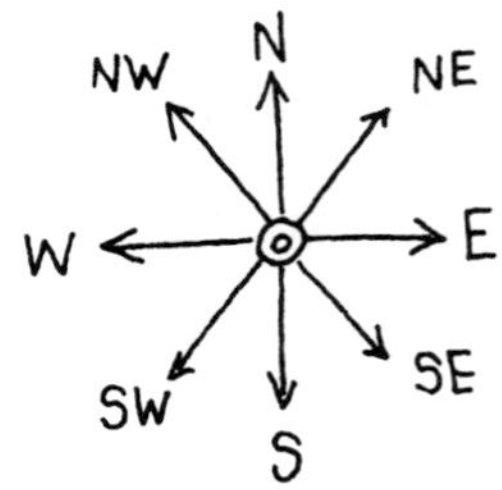

Example: There will be heavy snow falls in the north west.

1 Temperatures over high ground will drop below freezing overnight.

2 Mist and fog patches near the coast will clear during the day.

3 It will remain overcast in the west.

4 Northerly winds will reach gale force in the north east.

5 Some areas will have thunderstorms.

6 The centre of the country will have sunny periods and showers.

7 The rain will be heavy at times in the east.

8 In the south most areas will remain dry and sunny with temperatures of 25 degrees.

9 There will be sunny spells in the afternoon in the south east.

a

b

c

d

e

f

g

h

i

j

11 Definitions

Choose the answer on the right which best describes the words on the left.

1 a gale	a) a very light breeze b) a very strong wind
2 overcast	a) cloudy b) sunny
3 a shower	a) long period of rain b) short period of rain
4 temperature below freezing	a) very cold b) warm
5 sunny periods/spells	a) sun and cloud b) sunny all day
6 dry	a) rainy and wet b) not rainy
7 heavy snowfalls	a) a lot of snow b) a little snow
8 storms	a) rain b) rain with thunder and lightning

10 Holidays

CHOOSING A HOLIDAY

1 Match the pictures

Match the pictures to the types of holidays below.

a ______________________

b ______________________

c ______________________

d ______________________

e ______________________

f ______________________

package holiday	activity holiday	camping holiday
walking tour	cultural tour	cruise

2 Holiday brochures

Use the words underneath to fill in the gaps in these brochures.

1 'The blue of the ______________ and the blue of the sky. Delicious food and high class entertainment. ______________ every day to a different ______________'

sailing sea destination

2 'Relax completely as we take care of everything. Your ______________ is with a top airline and you'll stay in a five-star ______________. All ______________ and entertainment arranged so you can enjoy yourself.'

flight excursions hotel

3 'The outdoor holiday with clean and fully-equipped ______________. A separate area for each ______________ with full washing and cooking ______________.'

tent sites facilities

4 'Shakespeare Country. Visit the ______________ town of Stratford upon Avon. Time for ______________ buying. Evening ______________ to theatre.'

souvenir historic trip

5 'Enjoy Britain on ______________. We take care of the ______________ while you admire the beautiful ______________ in your own time.'

scenery foot luggage

6 'Something for everybody. Go ______________ on the waters of Lake Kuron, ______________ in the Welsh mountains or ______________ through the Black Forest.'

rock-climbing canoeing pony-trekking

THINGS TO DO ON HOLIDAY

3 Match them!

Choose the correct verb to complete each phrase.

go take write buy	get eat have speak	a foreign language postcards souvenirs a suntan a good time	sightseeing photos foreign food

4 Places to stay

1 If you have enough money you can stay in a five-star h___________l. **(teo)**
2 A c___________e is a much cheaper place to spend the night! **(sitamp)**
3 In America people use their cars to go on holiday and there are plenty of m___________s near the main highways **(lteo)**
4 A traditional and inexpensive place to stay in England is a b__d and b___________t **(e/kearsaf)**
5 Sometimes these are called g___________s. **(steusouhe)**
6 In some countries you can stay in a wooden house called a c___________t. **(lhea)**
7 With a c___________n you can take your home on holiday too! **(avarna)**

5 At the seaside

Label the picture using these words.

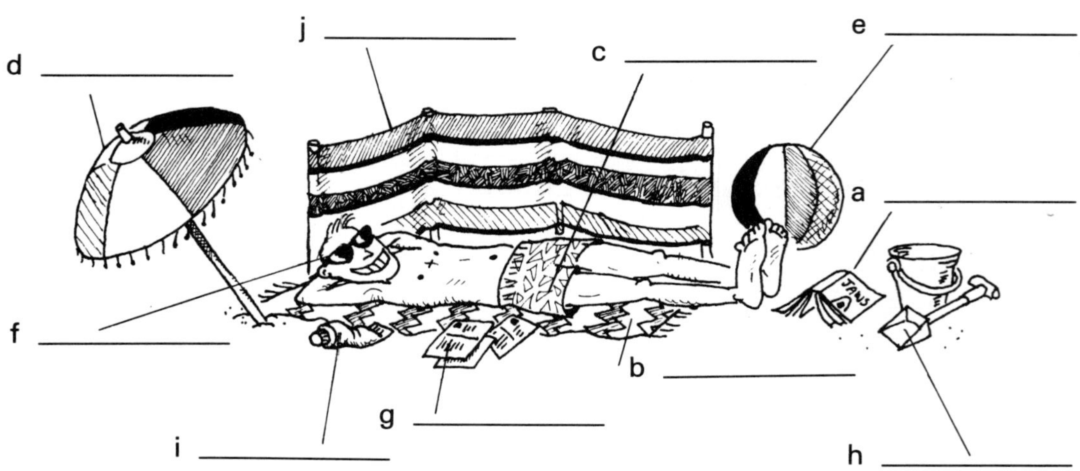

book	towel	swimsuit	umbrella	beachball	sunglasses
postcards	bucket and spade	suncream	windbreak		

AT THE HOTEL

6 What to do

Match the actions on the left with the pictures on the right.

1 catching the hotel bus ____

2 checking in at reception ____

3 giving the porter a tip ____

4 unpacking your suitcase ____

5 changing your traveller's cheques ____

6 sunbathing by the pool ____

7 dining in the hotel restaurant ____

8 ringing up for room service ____

a

b

c
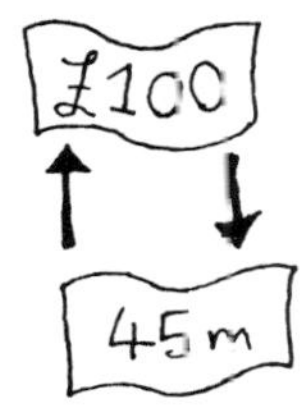

d

e

f

g

h

7 People who help

Fill in the missing letters to complete the names of these jobs.

1 A person who arranges people's holidays and journeys is a t__ a__el a__en__.
2 Someone who goes with tourists as they visit different places is a t__ __r l__ __d__r.
3 Someone who knows about and shows people a particular interesting place is a g__i__e.
4 Someone who works for a travel company and helps tourists at the hotel is a h__l__d__y repr__s__nt__ti__e.
5 Someone who looks after passengers on an aircraft is an __ir h__st__ss or a s__e__a__d.
6 Someone who helps people with their luggage at an airport, station, hotel etc is a p__ __t__r.

8 What are you?

Two of the three words in brackets can be used to complete each sentence below.

1 The beaches of Spain will be crowded this summer with a record number of foreign ______________. (*travellers/tourists/guests*)

2 The Channel Tunnel link between Britain and France will make journeys easier for ______________. (*visitors/guests/travellers*)

3 Who's that at the door? I'm not expecting any ______________ at this moment. (*tourists/visitors/guests*)

4 These motoring guides are excellent for ______________ here on holiday. (*foreigners/strangers/travellers*)

5 The local people dislike visits even from ______________ from their own country. (*foreigners/strangers/tourists*)

6 The hotel offered a wide range of services to all ______________ to the conference. (*guests/strangers/visitors*)

THE WORST HOLIDAY EVER!!

9 Conversation

Complete the dialogue with these phrases.

on strike	**sunstroke**	**delayed**	**lost**	**food poisoning**	**stolen**

A: Hi, Jenny. How was your holiday?
B: Hello, Vicky – oh I am so glad to be home!
A: Why, what happened?
B: Everything! It was the worst holiday ever. First the plane didn't leave the airport for three hours because the flight was **a)** ______________ by bad weather and then when we got there . . . .
A: What was the hotel like?
B: Great except the staff were **b)** ______________ because they hadn't been paid for two months!
A: Oh Jenny, how awful, what about David and the children?
B: Well, David spent all day on the beach and got **c)** ______________ and the children ate something horrible and got **d)** ______________.
A: It sounds terrible! Nothing else I hope?
B: No, apart from our last night at a disco. It was so dark that at the end we found our passports and money had been **e)** ______________ by thieves!!

A: I'm not surprised you were glad to get home!
B: Yes it was great until we landed and I discovered that our luggage had been
f) ____________ by the airline!!!

10 Public holidays

Find the following public holidays in the word puzzle.

1 A holiday in GB even if you don't work in one!
[B________ H________]

2 Springtime holiday when you might get a chocolate
egg! [E________]

3 First day of number 2 [G________ F________]

4 First day of the year [N________ Y________
D________]

5 The day before number 4 [N________
Y________ E________]

6 First of the fifth month – often a workers' holiday [M________ D________]

7 British children get presents on this day in December [C________ D________]

8 The day after number 7 [B________ D________]

9 Two days before number 8! [C________ E________]

C	H	R	I	S	T	M	A	S	D	A	Y
H	E	B	O	X	I	N	G	T	R	C	N
R	E	A	C	D	S	G	D	V	I	O	E
I	U	N	M	U	N	O	A	S	W	D	W
S	Q	K	S	U	P	O	Y	J	I	M	Y
T	E	H	O	L	I	D	A	Y	A	S	E
M	A	Y	D	A	Y	F	F	O	P	L	A
A	H	U	M	I	P	R	A	S	B	U	R
S	T	R	N	K	L	I	G	N	M	L	S
E	A	S	T	E	R	D	W	U	T	K	D
V	D	G	I	K	L	A	W	P	L	U	A
E	K	M	I	T	C	Y	F	J	A	O	Y
N	E	W	Y	E	A	R	S	E	V	E	L

11 A place to live

HOUSES

1 What kind of house?

Unscramble the words in the sentences below.

1 I live on the 20th floor of a b____________k of f____________s. In the mornings I use the stairs down but in the evenings I take the lift. **(col/alt)**

2 My home is a very pretty little c____________e in a small village far away from the nearest town. **(gatot)**

3 My family have lived in this f____________e for hundreds of years and we have always raised sheep and horses here too. **(ramuhso)**

4 This type of house is known as a s____________-d____________d because it shares one wall with another property. **(mie/echeat)**

5 A t____________d house has houses on both sides and is very common in the older parts of the city. **(recare)**

6 It's so convenient for my grandmother to have everything on the same floor so I think she's really happy in her b____________w. **(lowunga)**

7 It's a bit difficult to remember where our house is because they all look the same on this h____________g e____________e. **(inous/tast)**

8 My brother lives on a h____________t on the River Thames. **(bouseoa)**

Now match your answers to the pictures below.

a

b

c

d

e

f

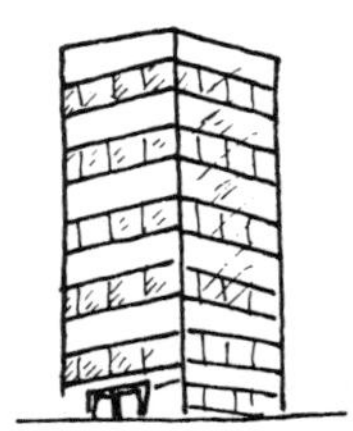

g

h

2 A new place

Match the actions to the pictures opposite. The pictures are in the right order to describe ways of getting a place ready to live in.

You build an extension. _____

You furnish the house. _____

You pull down old buildings. _____

You paint and decorate. _____

You put up new house. _____

a

b

c

d

e

YOUR HOUSE AND AREA

3 Exteriors

Read the texts and label the pictures with the words underlined.

The Front

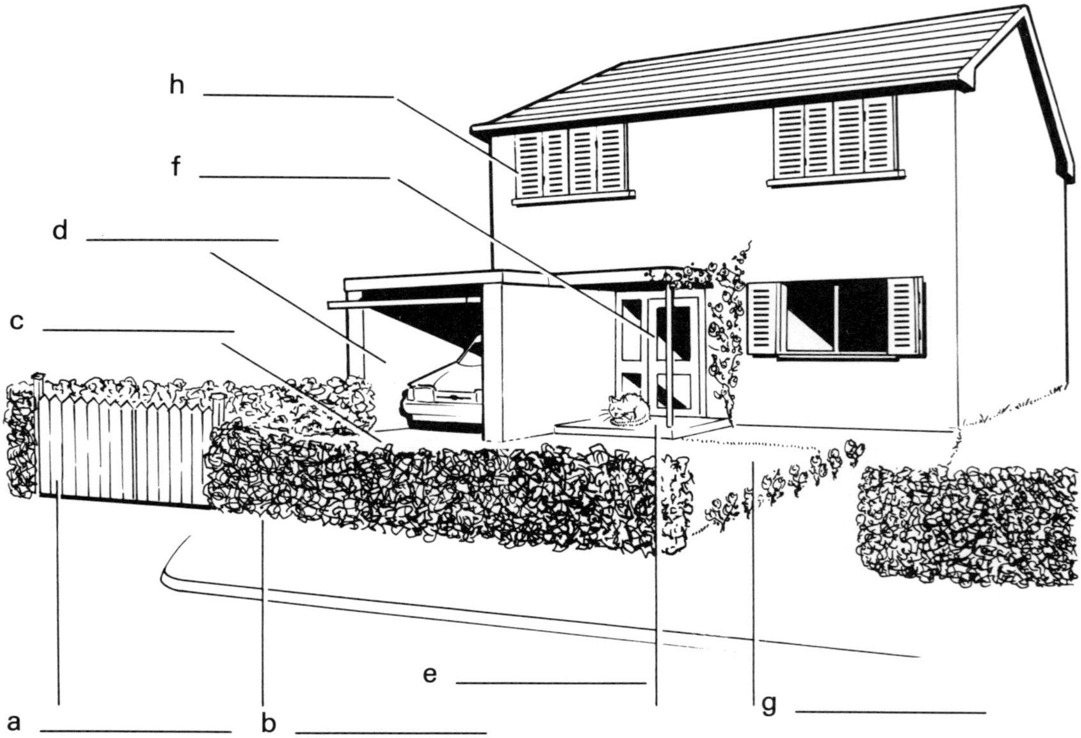

My house has roses growing around the front door and the cat is usually asleep on the doorstep when I come home. In the front garden there is a lovely green hedge which grows so quickly that sometimes I can't get my car through the gate and up the drive to the garage to the left of the house. Above the door the shutters of my bedroom are closed.

The Back

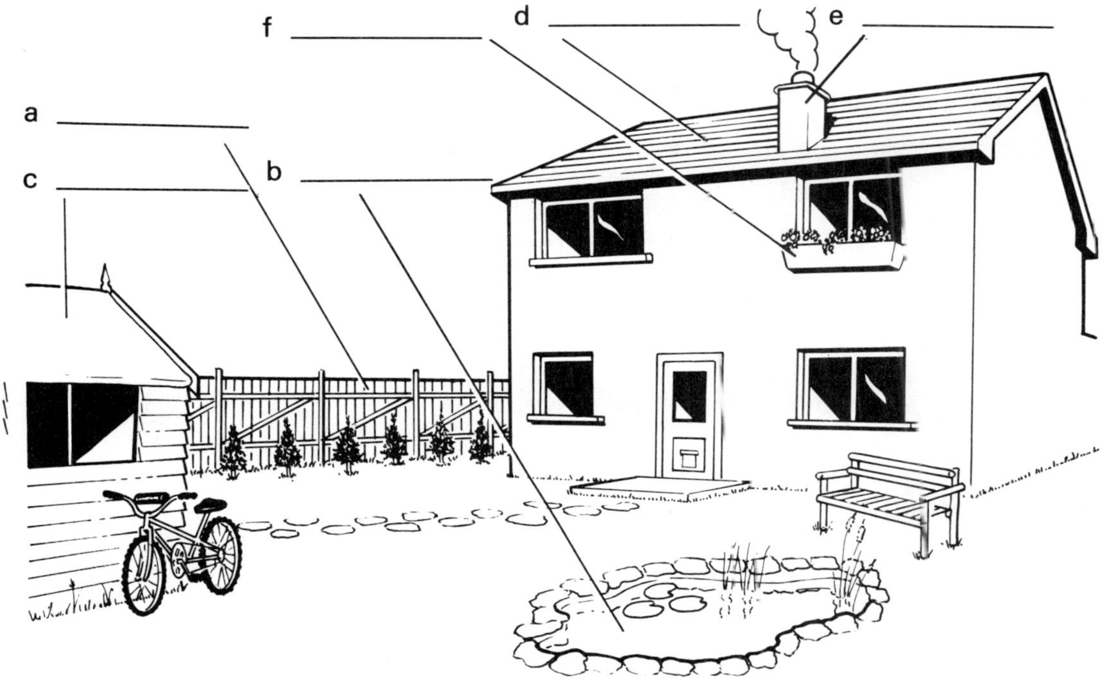

In the back garden we've built a garden pond with a little wooden bench next to it. We're trying to grow some small trees along the fence so that the neighbours can't see in. The garden shed needs tidying because the children play in it in the holidays. It's getting colder in the evenings now and I can see smoke coming out of the chimney on the roof which means there's a fire inside. On the window sill my wife has put some flowerpots with her favourite plants.

4 Areas

Complete the sentences using the word in brackets.

Example: An (INDUSTRY) area can be polluted because of all the large factories but at least I can get a job easily.

Answer: An **industrial** area can be polluted because of all the large factories but at least I can get a job easily.

1 Living in an (AGRICULTURE) area means a quiet life away from the city but it's nice to get fresh food from the farm. ____________

2 It takes half an hour by train from this (SUBURB) area to the city centre. ____________

3 I love living in the (COMMERCE) area as I can walk to my office and be near all the big shops too. ____________

4 It's almost all houses and flats in this (RESIDENT) area. ____________

5 Because it is a (COAST) town we can get fresh fish every day. ____________

6 Most cities have a (FINANCE) centre where the banks and insurance companies have their head offices. ____________

7 If you want to catch a train the main stations are in the (CENTRE) part of the city. ____________

TOWN OR COUNTRY

5 City sights

Label the pictures using the words underneath. Look up any words you don't know in your dictionary.

a ____________
b ____________
c ____________
d ____________
e ____________
f ____________
g ____________
h ____________
i ____________
j ____________

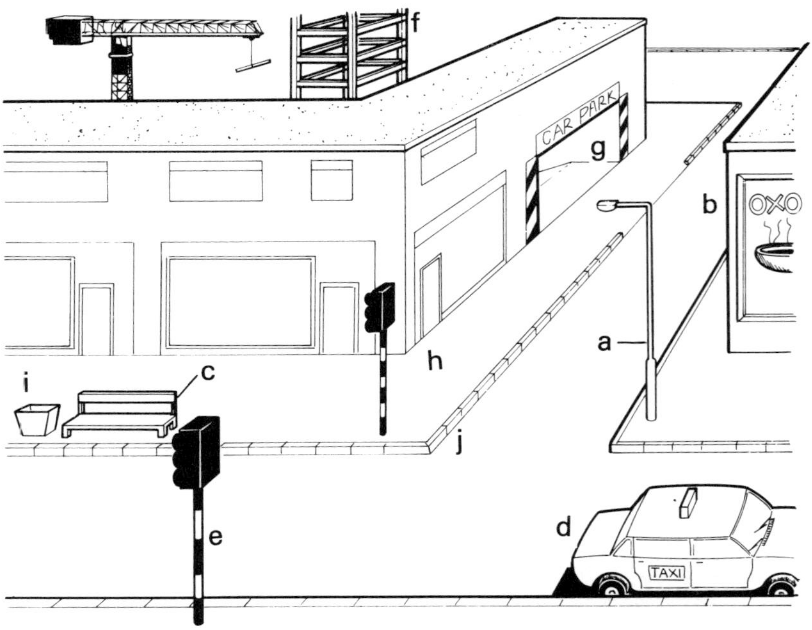

lamp post	advert	bench	taxi rank	traffic lights
building site	car park or parking meter	pavement		
litter bin	kerb			

6 Country sights

Label the pictures using the words underneath.

a ______________

b ______________

c ______________

d ______________

e ______________

f ______________

g ______________

h ______________

i ______________

j ______________

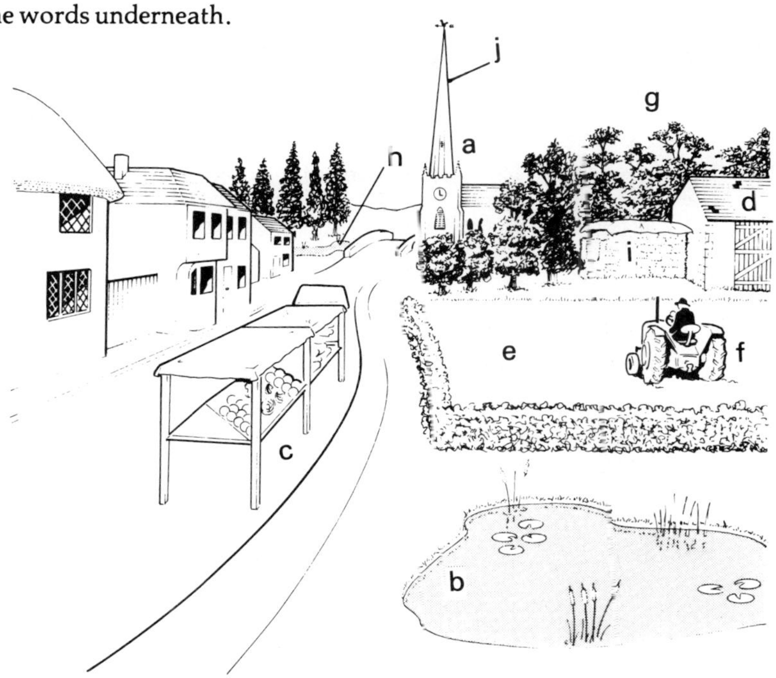

church	spire	village pond	market	barn	field
tractor	wood	stream	hay stack		

7 Complete the sentences

Unscramble the words to complete the sentences below.

1 It was impossible to go any further in the car so we got out and carried up the mountain **(hapt)** on foot. ______________

2 The policeman couldn't see the man any more and realised he must have disappeared down one of the **(selaly)** between the houses. ______________

3 You could see the farmer in the field leading the sheep down the **(crtak)** to the river. ______________

4 In the old part of the city there are lots of **(ealns)** full of interesting shops and restaurants. ______________

5 They walked along the nature **(irtal)** enjoying the fresh air and beautiful scenery. ______________

HOW DO YOU LIVE?

8 Owner or tenant?

Complete the conversations with these words.

mortgage borrow costs loan afford

A: Hello, Mr Brown. I understand you want to **(1)**____________ some money from the bank.
B: Yes, we want a **(2)**____________ to buy a house.
A: I see. What you want is a **(3)**____________.
B: I hope we can **(4)**____________ it.
A: Don't worry. It usually **(5)**____________ about the same as you are paying now.

renting landlady room tenant

C: Good afternoon. I'm Joe Lawrence from the University. I've come to see the **(6)**____________.
D: Come in and have a look. It's the one next to mine.
C: Oh, are you a **(7)**____________ here too?
D: Yes, I've been **(8)**____________ from Mrs Saunders for two years.
C: Is Mrs Saunders the **(9)**____________?
D: Yes, she's very friendly.

own survey lodger landlord

E: Good evening, sir. May I ask you a few questions?
F: What about? I'm in a hurry, I'm afraid.
E: We are doing a **(10)**____________ on housing. Do you **(11)**____________ a house or flat?
F: No, because of my job I am a **(12)**____________ at the moment.
E: That means you get your meals cooked, doesn't it?
F: Yes, although the **(13)**____________ thinks he is a better cook than he is!

estate agents move in keys contract

G: You look happy, Sue.
H: Yes, we're going to **(14)**____________ to our new house at the weekend.
G: Have you signed the **(15)**____________?
H: Yes, and I pick up the **(16)**____________ from the **(17)**____________ tomorrow.

12 Spare time

HOBBIES

1 Match them!

Match the verbs on the left with the phrases on the right.

You can	1 learn	a stamps
	2 take	b music
	3 paint	c voluntary work
	4 grow	d sailing
	5 go	e a language
	6 collect	f pictures
	7 watch	g vegetables
	8 do	h photographs
	9 listen to	i football

2 What else can you do?

Can you think of other things you do? Complete these word families with suitable answers. You may find a dictionary helpful.

a learn a language
to sew
____
____

b collect stamps
postcards
____
____

c grow vegetables
herbs
____
____

d watch football
cricket
____
____

e listen to classical music
opera
____
____

f play the piano
squash
____
____

3 People

What do you call someone who _____?

If you learn a language you are a learn<u>er</u>.

Can you make similar nouns from these verbs? Be careful! One of the answers is spelt differently.

to paint	a ______________
to garden	a ______________
to collect	a ______________
to watch	a ______________
to listen	a ______________

EQUIPMENT

4 What do you need?

Below is some of the equipment you need to do these four hobbies. Which two are needed for each hobby? Use your dictionary if necessary.

GARDENING	PHOTOGRAPHY	CAR MAINTENANCE	BIRD WATCHING
______________	______________	______________	______________
______________	______________	______________	______________

spade camera spanner film can of oil pocket guide
packet of seeds binoculars

5 Missing letters

Here is a list of other hobbies and the equipment you need. Can you fill in the missing letters?

Jogging	Do it yourself	Cooking
r__nn__ng __ho__s	t____ls	r__ci__es
tr__ck s____t	woo__	m__x__ng b__wl

WHICH TO CHOOSE?

6 Same or different

Read the passage below and find words or phrases underlined in the text that mean:

a the *same* as:

1 active ____________

2 liked by many people ____________

3 cheap ____________

4 preferred ____________

5 friendly ____________

6 restful ____________

and **b** the *opposite* of:

7 boring ____________

8 unhealthy ____________

9 safe ____________

A: What kinds of activities do you recommend for people without much money?
B: An inexpensive hobby is jogging. All you really need is a good pair of running shoes. It will keep you fit too – lots of fresh air and exercise is so good for you.
A: How about people who are not so energetic?
B: You can always watch rather than play – spectator sports like football and tennis are popular. It's better to go to the matches than see them on TV. But if you really want something exciting then try an outdoor activity like rock climbing, parachuting or hang gliding. But be careful because these are all fairly dangerous – you must learn how to do them without hurting yourself.
A: Is there a good way of getting to know people through a hobby?
B: Yes. My favourite pastime is playing squash and I belong to a club. After the game I have time to be sociable with the other members.
A: Let's finish with something more relaxing.
B: Well after a hard day's work some people like painting, reading or listening to music and I suppose there's always the television.

7 Find the hobby

Which of these hobbies or pastimes are mentioned in Exercise 6? Write them under the pictures below. There is one extra picture. Can you find it and describe the activity?

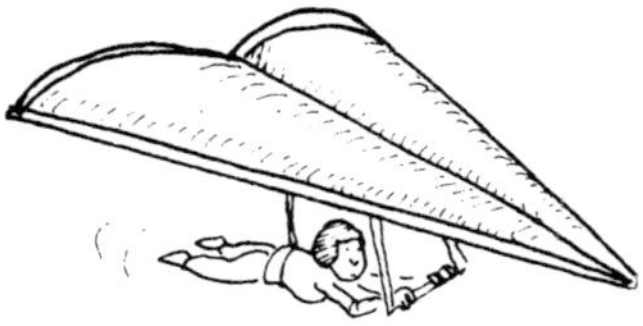

a ____________

b ____________

c ____________

d ____________

e ____________

f ____________

g ____________

h ____________

i ____________

j ____________

k ____________

l ____________

GOING OUT, STAYING IN

8 Where to go on a Saturday night?

Can you find the names of the following places in this word puzzle?

1 Somewhere open late at night where you can see a show or have a dance n____________

2 Somewhere with a stage where you can watch a play	t__________
3 A place to watch films	c__________
4 Somewhere to listen to music	c_____ h_____
5 A place to dance to music	d__________
6 A place to see shows of dancing, singing and comedy	c__________
7 A place to watch dancing	b__________
8 A place to have a drink	b__________

C	I	N	E	M	A	G	R	O	N	A
A	B	I	F	U	S	H	X	M	T	D
B	D	G	S	Y	B	A	L	L	E	T
A	D	H	T	A	C	M	K	P	F	H
R	I	T	E	G	O	R	S	G	Z	E
E	S	C	O	N	C	E	R	T	U	A
T	M	L	A	N	F	L	E	H	I	T
H	D	U	S	Y	M	K	G	A	D	R
P	S	B	O	T	I	L	A	L	T	E
D	Y	E	P	R	E	Q	A	L	W	D

9 Staying in tonight?

What is there to watch on TV? Complete the TV guide using these words.

Documentary	News	Soap opera	Quiz show
Detective series	Sports		

6.00 **a)** __________

All the latest from around the world

6.30 **c)** __________

Win a car or a holiday in our fun game!

7.00 **e)** __________

A report on the increase in crime in the UK

8.00 **b)** __________

Football action from the top games in Division 1

9.00 **d)** __________

Can Sherlock Holmes catch the drug dealers?

10.00 **f)** __________

Everyday life of the most famous family in France

13 Arts and entertainment

PERFORMERS

1 Who does what?

Fill in the missing letters to complete the names of these people and match them to the pictures.

a ______________ b ______________ c ______________ d ______________

e ______________ f ______________ g ______________

1 art__st
2 co__ __oser
3 auth__ __
4 __ct__r
5 con__ucto__
6 __usi__ian
7 d__nc__r

2 What do they do?

Make 6 sentences saying what these people do. Use the verbs and nouns below.

writes/performs/conducts writes/paints/plays plays	pictures/dances/a role the orchestra/books/music an instrument/

Example: An actor plays a role.

1 An author ______________________________

2 A dancer ______________________________

3 A conductor ______________________________

4 A composer ______________________________

5 An artist ______________________________

6 A musician ______________________________

3 The world of film

Find the definitions in the word puzzle.

1 People who are famous for their work in films s__________

2 The person in charge of the making of the film d__________

3 A film that tries to frighten the audience h__________ f__________

4 What you look at in the cinema s__________

5 A film about a romantic relationship l______ s______

6 The words that a particular actor says l__________

7 A film that tries to make the audience laugh c__________

8 The person who finds the money to make a film p__________

9 A film with songs m__________

D	I	R	E	C	T	O	R	C	N
S	L	M	K	S	T	V	X	O	M
P	A	T	S	T	U	R	A	M	U
C	E	M	C	A	H	I	V	E	S
J	H	O	R	R	Y	N	T	D	I
L	O	V	E	S	T	O	R	Y	C
I	R	W	E	C	B	M	T	G	A
N	R	E	N	T	L	E	K	I	L
E	O	P	R	O	D	U	C	E	R
S	R	F	I	L	M	T	R	A	M

BOOKS

4 What are you reading?

Unscramble the letters to describe these different types of books.

1 She was born on 1 January 1900 to a poor Scottish family. **(grioaph)** B__________y

2 Debra turned to Rodney and looked in his eyes. 'I love you' she whispered. **(antomi/eov)** R__________c N__________l

3 I must go down to the seas again, to the lonely sea and the sky
And all I want is a tall ship and a star to steer her by. **(erto)** P__________y

4 I'm sure this is the knife that killed her. Take it back to the police station and check it for fingerprints. **(vietetc/rto)** D__________e S__________y

5 . . . . so the wicked giant was dead. The princess married the handsome prince and they all lived happily ever after. **(ira/rot)** F__________y S__________y

6 My earliest memories are of my first school. I started in Miss Brown's class. **(tougarobiph)** A__________y

7 He tried to undo the ropes that held him to the chair. All he could hear was the sound of the train getting nearer and nearer. **(lerhil)** T__________r

8 Brighton is a lively seaside town. **(erav/dui)** T__________l G__________e

9 In 1844 the Government decided to create a National Savings bank. **(ootexb)** T__________k

5 Fiction and non-fiction

Fit the types of books in Exercise 4 into the diagram below.

Fiction (imaginary)	Non-fiction (factual)
poetry	textbook
________	biography
________	________
________	________
________	
________	

THEATRE

6 An evening at the theatre

Put the sentences below into the correct order.

1 The first appearance of the actors was greeted by tremendous clapping from the audience. ____

2 It was the first night of a new play and when we arrived there was already a large crowd on the steps of the theatre. ____

3 During the interval we had ice-creams in the bar. ____

4 We joined the long queue to get our tickets that we had booked two months before. ____

5 The theatre was very full but everyone stopped talking as the curtain went up. ____

6 The last scene was excellent and the audience shouted excitedly until the actors came back on the stage. ____

7 We bought a programme in the entrance hall and read about the actors and the story of the play. ____

8 We found our seats in the front row very close to the stage. ____

7 Definitions

Match the words underlined in Exercise 6 with the definitions below.

1 A piece of writing for the theatre. __________
2 A small booklet that gives details about the show. __________
3 A line of seats. __________
4 People who pay to watch something. __________
5 The place where the actors stand. __________
6 A piece of material at the front of the stage. __________
7 Making a noise with your hands to show you like something. __________
8 Time between the parts of the show. __________
9 A place in a theatre to get something to eat or drink. __________
10 A line of waiting people. __________
11 Asked for tickets some time before the show. __________
12 The first time a show is presented to the public. __________

MUSIC

8 Instrumental music

Label the pictures with the names of the instruments below.

drums	guitar	violin	piano	trumpet	organ	saxophone

a __________

b __________

c __________

d __________

e __________

f __________

g __________

9 Musicians

What do you call someone who plays one of the instruments in Exercise 8? Be careful with the spelling!

-ist	-er
a guitarist	a drummer
____________	____________
____________	____________
____________	____________
____________	____________

10 Music at home

Label the items in the picture using the words below.

a ____________

b ____________

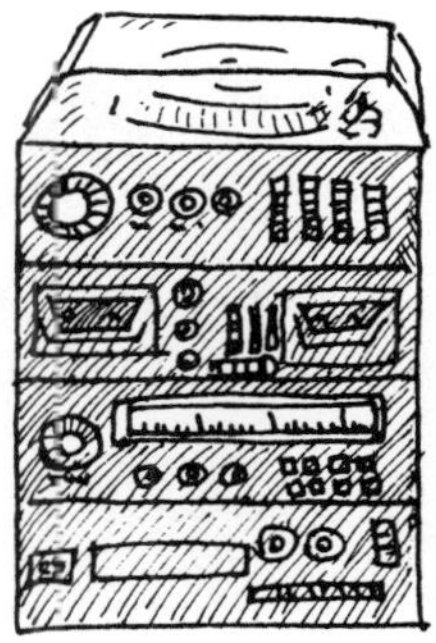

c ____________

d ____________

e ____________

f ____________

g ____________

hi-fi or stereo	record player	album	compact disc
loudspeaker	cassette	headphones	

14 Emotions

FEELINGS

1 How do you feel?

Look at these situations and match the emotions to the pictures.

1 Someone has just damaged your new car. _____

2 Your pet dog has died. _____

3 Your friend has won a lot of money. _____

4 You have received a long letter from your best friend. _____

5 You've eaten all the chocolates in the box. _____

6 You don't know what is behind the door. _____

a sadness
b fear
c anger
d envy
e greed
f pleasure

Now make adjectives from the nouns.

Example: I feel very __angry__ **(anger)**.

7 I feel very ________________ **(sadness)**
8 I feel very ________________ **(envy)**
9 I feel very ________________ **(pleasure)**
10 I feel very ________________ **(greed)**
11 I feel very ________________ **(fear)**

WHAT DO YOU THINK?

2 Opinions

Can you fill in the missing letters?

To h__ __ __ (to have an extremely strong and negative feeling about someone or something)

To d__s__ __k__ (to think someone or something is not pleasant)

To d__s__pp__ __v__ of (to think something is not the right way to act)

To be f__n__ of (to like a person or action)

To a__ __rec__ __te (to realise the value of someone or something)

To l__v__ (to have strong and positive feelings)

Now complete these sentences with a suitable verb from page 79.

1 I ______________ people who smoke in restaurants when others are eating.
2 I have ______________ you deeply since the day we first met and I want to marry you.
3 I am ______________ my Uncle Philip because he is a patient and generous man.
4 I ______________ working with him because he is always telling me that I am wrong.
5 I saw him standing over the body and realised that I ______________ him enough to kill him with my own hands.
6 I ______________ my music teacher because she worked very hard for all the children.

PEOPLE

3 Friends or enemies?

Look in the word puzzle on page 81 for the words that fit the following definitions.

1 someone who has done things that other people think are brave and good h______________
2 someone you like spending time with c______________
3 someone who does not tell you the truth l______________
4 someone that you work with c______________
5 someone that you are fighting against e______________
6 someone who runs away instead of fighting c______________
7 someone who is against you in a game or argument o______________
8 someone that you like f______________

S	Q	K	A	F	B	R	U	T	C
V	O	H	E	R	O	Z	H	X	O
L	T	P	S	I	R	B	E	F	M
C	A	T	R	E	L	S	N	P	P
O	P	P	O	N	E	N	T	E	A
W	Y	E	N	D	R	H	F	A	N
A	P	E	N	E	M	Y	L	M	I
R	S	T	L	I	A	R	X	G	O
D	A	B	E	F	O	L	M	N	N
C	O	L	L	E	A	G	U	E	N

WHAT ARE THEY LIKE?

4 Similar but different

Complete the sentences below using ONE from each pair of words above them.

foolish or **brave**?

1a Everyone said how _____________ the young woman was to keep the gunman talking until the police arrived and she was given a special medal.

1b I think she was _____________ to put herself in danger because it is the job of trained people to handle these situations.

polite or **decent**?

2a It was very _____________ of you to help that old lady with her problems with her landlord.

2b I think it is only _____________ to listen to other people first before you say what you think.

nervous or **worried**?

3a Sue had been bitten by a dog when she was very young and was always ______________ of all of our animals.

3b Many scientists are very ______________ about the effects of the increase in the world population.

sensitive or **sensible**?

4a He is always ______________ about driving in the rain and never goes too fast.

4b Max was a poet who did not like criticism and was very ______________ about his writing.

jealous or **envious**?

5a I am ______________ of anyone who finds it easy to learn to speak another language.

5b I was ______________ of my brother because he always seemed to get better presents than me.

greedy or **selfish**?

6a She was such a ______________ person that she smoked throughout the meal without asking.

6b He was very ______________ and insisted on trying every dish on the menu.

15 Clothes

WHAT ARE THEY WEARING?

1 Name these clothes

Fill in the missing letters and label the pictures.

h__t	c__p	gl__v__s	sh__rt
sk__ __t	j__m__er	c__ __t	jack__t } su__t
bl__ __se	sh__ __ts	j__ __ns	tr__ __sers } su__t
sh__ __s	s__cks	b__ __ts	t__e
gl__ss__s	tr__ __ners	st__ck	h__ndk__rch__ __f

2 Underwear

Label these pictures in the same way.

b__a

kn__ck__rs

t__ __hts

ve__t

un__ __rp__nts

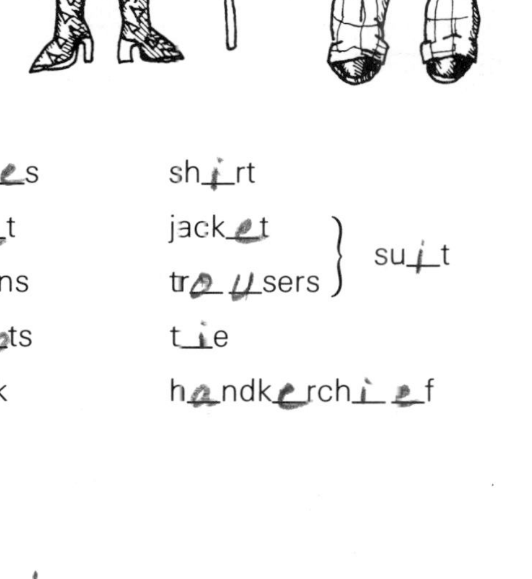

3 Patterns and designs

Look at these sentences about the clothing in Exercises 1 and 2.

1 Julie is wearing a plain skirt and a floral blouse.
2 Brian is wearing a hooped jumper.
3 Annie is wearing a tartan scarf and patterned boots.
4 Iain is wearing a checked suit, a striped shirt and a polka-dot handkerchief and tie.

Now match the patterns and designs to the words below. The first one has been done for you.

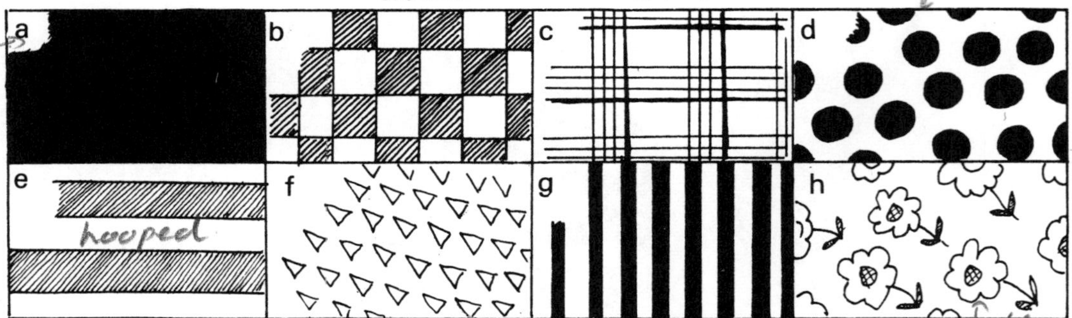

plain	striped	hooped	patterned	checked	tartan
floral	polka-dot				

a plain ______ b ______ c ______ d ______
e ______ f ______ g ______ h ______

ACCESSORIES

4 The well-dressed woman

Look at these word pictures and fill in the names.

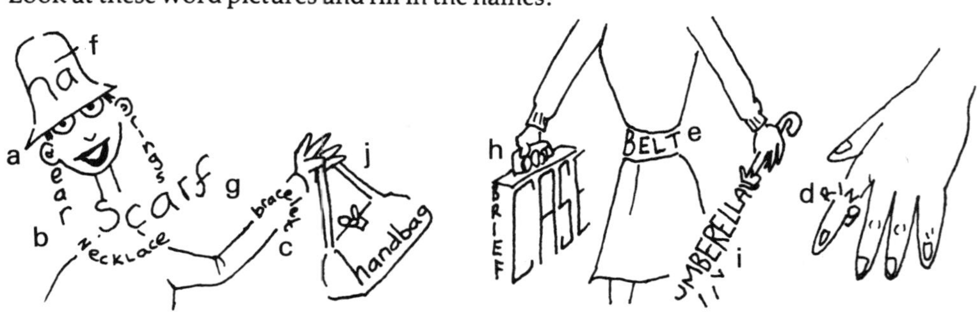

a earring
b necklace
c bracelet
d ring
e belt
f hat
g scarf
h briefcase
i umbrella
j handbag

5 Carry or wear?

Look at these examples and then look at Exercise **4** again.

She was wearing a light summer dress because it was a warm day.
She carried her umbrella as it was not raining.

Now put the rest of the items in the picture into the right category.

Wear	Carry
a skirt	an umbrella
	briefcase
	handbag

6 What's it made of?

Look at Exercise **4** and complete the sentences using these words.

cotton	nylon	gold	silver	wool
	leather	silk	straw	
	cuir	soie	paille	

1 Her belt and briefcase are made of leather.
2 Her earrings and bracelet are made of silver.
3 Her wedding ring is made of gold.
4 Her summer skirt is made of cotton.
5 Her scarf is expensive and is made of silk.

6 Her jumper is made of wool.
7 Her hat is made of straw.
8 Her umbrella is made of nylon.

SHOPPING

7 Buying a new coat

Put the phrases on the left in the same order as the pictures on the right.

Try the coat on 4
Choose a coat 2
Ask for your size 1
Pay for the coat 6
Take the coat off 5
Ask about the price 3

1

2

3

4

5

6

8 Moneybags

Unscramble the letters in brackets to complete the sentences.

1 Many British women carry a h<u>an ba</u>g for their chequebook, keys, diaries and other things. **(danba)**

2 They usually have a p<u>urs</u>e to keep their money in. **(rsu)**

3 Most British men prefer to have a w<u>alle</u>t which they often keep in an inside pocket of their coat or jacket. **(leal)**

9 Similar but different

Complete these sentences by using each word once only.

price or **cost**?

1a Look at the ticket on that jacket. I haven't got my glasses and I can't read the price.

1b She had her dress made especially for the Royal visit and the total cost of her outfit was over £1,000!

worth or **value**?

2a I am sure my mother's wedding dress is worth a lot of money although I will never sell it.

2b Diamond rings never lose their value and are often bought as investments.

bargain or **second-hand**?

3a He was very poor and could not afford anything new so all his clothes were second-hand.

3b Now the hot weather is over it is a good time to go shopping for a bargain because all the shops are selling their light clothes at low prices.

GIVE YOURSELF A TREAT

10 In a shop

Look at these verbs and their meanings. Then complete the conversation below.

to alter = to change
to fit = to be the correct size
to shorten = to make shorter
to match = to be the same colour
to measure = to find out the correct size
to suit = to be the right style for someone

Customer:	Could you help me? I am looking for a cotton skirt.
Shop Assistant:	Certainly. What size are you?
Customer:	I've no idea, I'm afraid.
Shop Assistant:	Just a minute, I'll **a)** measure you.
Customer:	Thank you very much
Shop Assistant:	You're size 14. What colour are you looking for?
Customer:	Something to **b)** match this blouse.

Shop Assistant:	I see. It's a light blue, isn't it? How about this one? There's a changing room over there.
Shop Assistant:	Does it **c)** fit ?
Customer:	It's a little too large around the waist. Can you **d)** alter it?
Shop Assistant:	Yes, of course.
Customer:	It's also longer than my coat.
Shop Assistant:	Well, we can **e)** shorten it for you too. It certainly **f)** suit you. You look lovely.

11 Making up

Look at the word picture.

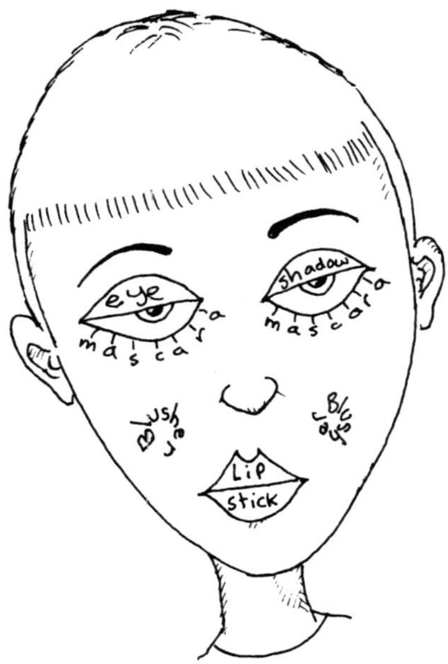

What different types of make-up can you see?

1 eye shadow　　　3 blusher
2 mascara　　　4 lipstick.

16 Crime and punishment

CRIME AND CRIMINALS

1 A court of law

Read this text and then use the underlined words to label the picture.

This is a court of law. In this room legal decisions are made. There is a large seat for the judge who wears special clothes to show that he has an important position. He must help the jury with questions about the law and how they must decide about the case. The twelve members of the jury sit together in two lines at the side of the court. Opposite the judge are two tables for the lawyers who argue about the facts of the case. There are usually at least two lawyers and one of them speaks for the accused. This is the man or woman that the police think has done something wrong. He or she must stand in a special place called the dock. The lawyers also question any witnesses. Witnesses have come to say what they have seen or know and they stand in the witness box.

2 Who did it?

Many of the words we use to describe criminals end in '-er'. Look at these two sentences:

Example: He was a **(murder)** who had killed a man without any reason.
Answer: He was a **murderer** who had killed a man without any reason.

Now make the criminal from the word in brackets in these sentences.

1 The **(rob)** took all the jewellery and money from the bank safe. ____________

2 The old lady was a **(shoplift)** who tried to leave without paying for all the things in her bag. ____________

3 She was still crying after the **(attack)** hit her and knocked her to the ground. ____________

4 All the passengers on the plane were frightened as the **(hijack)** pointed a gun at the pilot and told him to land. ____________

5 The **(smuggle)** hid the drugs in her handbag but the police dog discovered them. ____________

CATCHING THE CRIMINAL

3 Bank robbery – the crime

Put the actions on the left in the right order by matching them to the pictures on the right.

Robbing the safe _____

Gang plotting the crime _____

Leaving a look-out _____

Getting away from the bank _____

Stealing a getaway car _____

a

b

c

d

e

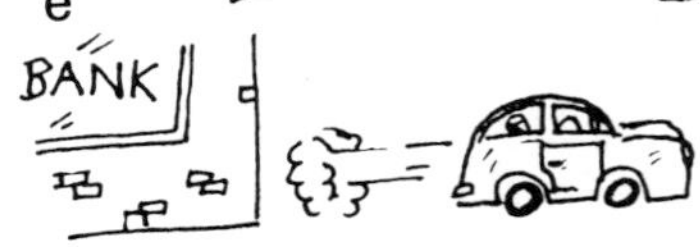

4 Bank robbery – the investigation

Put the actions on the left in the right order by matching them to the pictures on the right.

Identifying the suspects _____

Chasing the gang _____

Interviewing witnesses _____

Arresting the suspects _____

Searching for clues _____

5 Fill in the gaps

Now use the words below to fill in the gaps in these sentences. The words can only be used once.

rob	steal	clue	suspect	witness	identify	interview
chase	search for	get away				

1 The criminals planned to ____________ the bank by pretending to be policemen.
2 The police want to ____________ anyone who saw the accident.
3 When the policeman saw the thief he began to ____________ him through the town.
4 The woman was so tall that it was easy for the ____________ to ____________ her.
5 If you leave your car open someone will try to ____________ it.
6 The police thought that the foreign passport they had found was a very important ____________.
7 Many criminals ____________ their next crime while they are in prison.
8 The police are looking for a ____________ who has long blond hair and very dark blue eyes and is very dangerous.
9 The gang ran out of the bank and were able to ____________ on motorcycles.
10 The police sometimes use dogs to help ____________ missing people.

LAW-MAKERS

6 Equipment

Unscramble the letters to name the policemen's equipment.

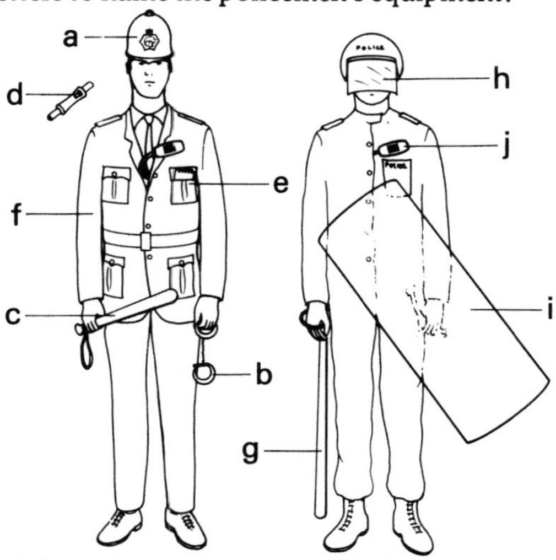

a h__________t **(meel)**

b h__________s **(dancfuf)**

c t__________n **(echonru)**

d w__________e **(ltish)**

e n__________k **(booote)**

f u__________m **(irofn)**

g b__________n **(ato)**

h v__________r **(sio)**

i r__________t s__________d **(io/ielh)**

j r__________o **(dia)**

7 Who does what?

Unscramble the letters to complete these sentences about people whose jobs involve the law.

1 When you join the police you normally start as a c__________e. **(stonabl)**

2 The police who investigate crimes after they occur are called d__________s. **(eetivect)**

3 There is a special d__________g s__________d who try to catch people like heroin dealers. **(ur/uqa)**

4 T__________c w__________s make sure that cars are not parked illegally. **(ffiar/denar)**

5 If you want some legal advice you can ask a s__________r. **(licitoo)**

8 Motoring offences

Match the pictures on the right with the motoring offences listed on the left.

Parking illegally _____

Speeding _____

Drunk driving _____

Leaving the scene of an accident _____

Driving dangerously _____

a

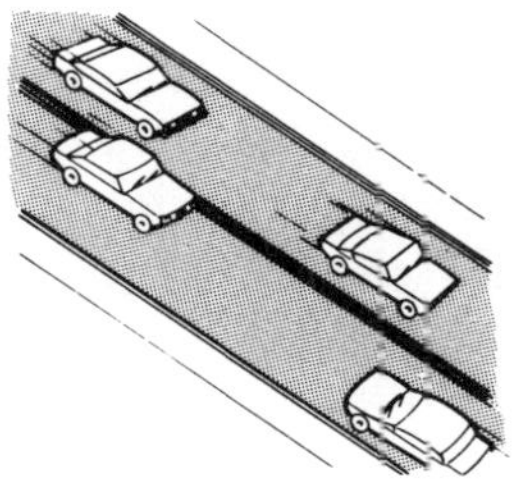

b

c

d

e

INNOCENT OR GUILTY?

9 What's going to happen?

If you have done something wrong there are usually two things a court can make you do.

The most important part of a trial is when the judge and jury decide whether the accused is guilty or not guilty. This is called the verdict. The acquittal of an innocent person means he or she is immediately released and can go home. A guilty person however must wait for the judge to decide the sentence. If the conviction is for a serious crime then the judge can send the person to prison although when it is the first offence the judge can choose to fine him or her instead. If they are good prisoners then they may be released early on parole but they must not commit another crime.

Find the underlined word in the passage that means:

1 a legal test ______________
2 the decision of the jury and judge ______________
3 what happens when someone is not guilty ______________
4 allowed to leave the court ______________
5 the punishment of the court ______________
6 the decision that someone is guilty ______________
7 a crime ______________
8 money that a guilty person may be ordered to pay ______________
9 allowed to leave prison before the end of your sentence ______________
10 to carry out a crime ______________

17 Education

EDUCATION IN BRITAIN

1 Schooldays

Answer the questions below using some of the underlined words.

Children can start school at 3 or 4 if there is a play school near their house. All children start primary school by the age of 5. If their parents want to pay for their school they can attend a private school but all children have the right to go to a state school. Later they will go to a secondary school until they are 16 or 18. If they do not want to stop they can continue their further education at a university or polytechnic where they will study academic subjects. They can also go to a college where they can study more practical subjects like art or engineering.

1 What is the first school a child can go to? ____________________

2 If your child is 7 years old what sort of school is s/he attending? ____________________

3 What sort of schools are free? ____________________

4 When can you leave a secondary school? ____________________

5 Where does someone go to study dressmaking? ____________________

2 What have you got today?

Write the words in the box in the pictures on the timetable.

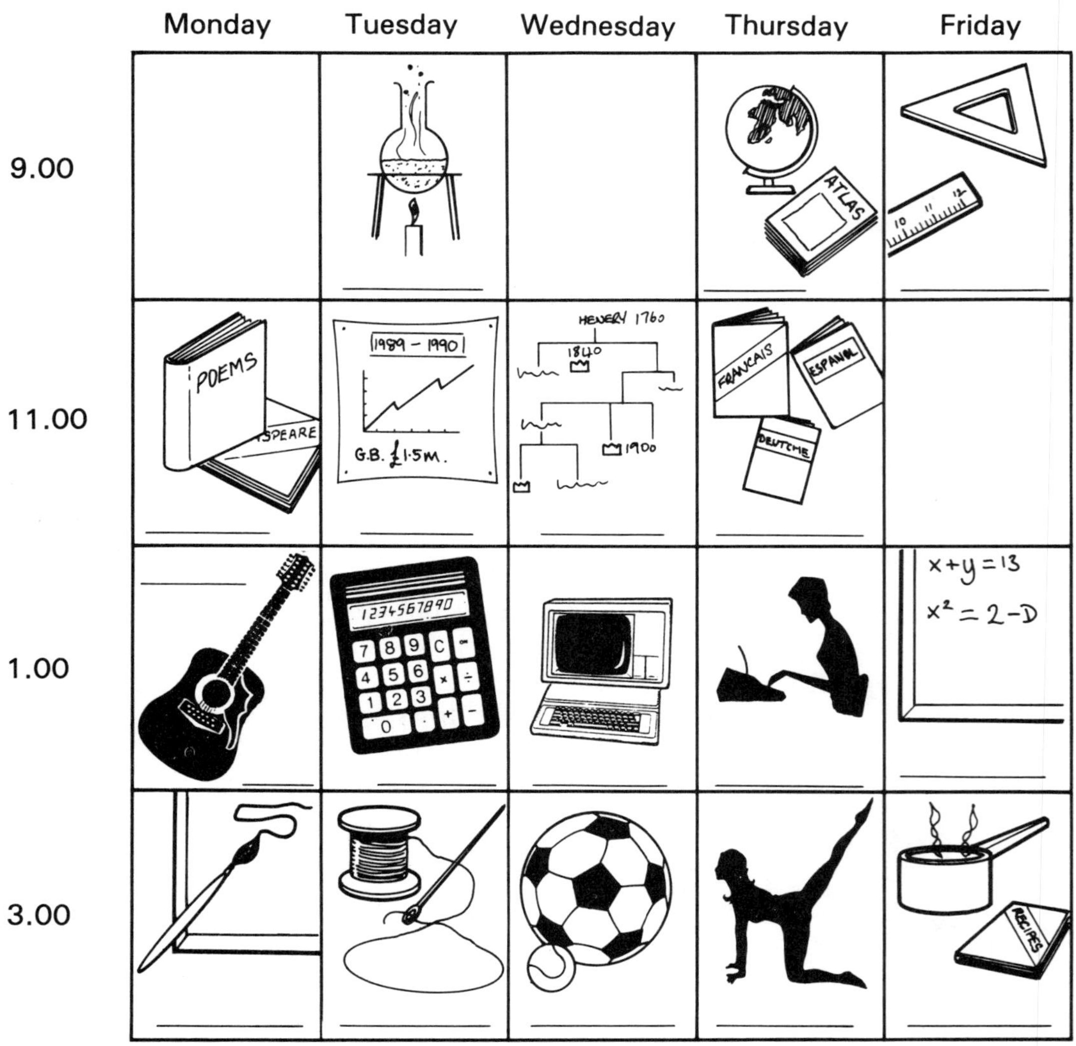

Art	Maths	History	Geography	Sport	Languages	Science
Literature	Technical Drawing	Typing	Economics	Cookery		
Sewing	Physical Education	Algebra	Music			
Computer Studies						

THE CLASSROOM

3 Name the objects

Label the objects in this picture with the underlined words in the passage:

The children are sitting behind their desks in rows facing the teacher who is writing on a large board with a piece of chalk. On her table is a pile of exercise books and textbooks. Later the children will put them in their bags to do their homework that evening. Some of them are writing in their books with their pens. Some of them are drawing in their books with a pencil. They are using their rulers to draw straight lines. If they make a mistake they can remove it with their rubbers. On the wall there are some wallcharts and a timetable.

a ________________	e ________________	i ________________
b ________________	f ________________	j ________________
c ________________	g ________________	k ________________
d ________________	h ________________	l ________________

HOW DO YOU LEARN?

4 Still using your fingers?

What do people say? Which words fit which pictures?

1 $\sqrt{9} = 3$

2 $4^4 = 16$

3 $17 + 3 = 20$

4 $4 \times 8 = 32$

5 10 % of 20 = 2

6 $8 \div 4 = 2$

plus	divided by	square root of
times	squared	per cent

Now complete the sentences using these words.

7 120 ____________ 80 equals 200
8 100 ____________ 5 equals 20
9 3 ____________ 15 equals 45
10 ____________ 81 equals 9
11 4 ____________ equals 16
12 50 ____________ of 50 equals 25

5 Scrambled words

Unscramble the letters in brackets to complete the sentences.

1 He has a vast k____________e of English history. **(wlegdno)**
2 L____________g gets more difficult as you get older. **(inearn)**
3 The e____________n in American schools is more modern than in the UK and every classroom has a computer in it. **(itoduca)**
4 Parents should share the u____________g of their children. **(pinbring)**
5 Some people question whether i____________e can be learnt at school. **(ncetelling)**

SUCCESS!

6 What do you get?

1 If you pass your driving test you get a ______________________________

2 If you pass your university exams you get a ______________________________

3 If you finish a training course you get a ______________________________

7 Exams

Match the verbs on the left with the definitions on the right. One has been done for you.

take	be successful
pass	learn about a subject
fail	do a test a second time
retake	do a test to show your knowledge of a subject
Study for	be unsuccessful

Wordlist

A		Unit
academic	/ ækəˈdemɪk /	17
accept	/ əkˈsept /	2
acceptance	/ əkˈseptəns /	2
accident	/ ˈæksɪdənt /	16
accused	/ əkˈju:zd /	16
acquittal	/ əˈkwɪtəl /	16
activity	/ ækˈtɪvɪtɪ /	10
actor	/ ˈæktə /	13
add	/ æd /	5
address	/ əˈdres /	2
adult	/ ˈædʌlt /	4
advertise	/ ˈædvətaɪz /	2
advertisement	/ ədˈvɜ:tɪsmənt /	2
afford	/ əˈfɔ:d /	11
afraid	/ əˈfreɪd /	13
agricultural	/ ægrɪˈkʌltʃərəl /	11
air hostess	/ ˈeə həʊstəs /	10
airport	/ ˈeəpɔ:t /	1
air steward	/ ˈeə stju:əd /	10
album cover	/ ˈælbʊm kʌvə /	13
algebra	/ ˈældʒəbrə /	17
alley	/ ˈæli: /	11
alter	/ ˈɔ:ltə /	15
anger	/ ˈæŋgə /	7
ankle	/ ˈæŋkəl /	13
angry	/ ˈæŋgri: /	13
application	/ æplɪˈkeɪʃən /	2
apply	/ əˈplaɪ /	2
appreciate	/ əˈpri:ʃɪeɪt /	13
April	/ ˈeɪprɪl /	9
argument	/ ˈɑ:gjʊmənt /	13
arm	/ ɑ:m /	7
arrange	/ əˈreɪndʒ /	2
arrangement	/ əˈreɪndʒmənt /	2
arrest	/ əˈrest /	16
art	/ ɑ:t /	17
artist	/ ˈɑ:tɪst /	13
ask	/ ɑ:sk /	15
attack	/ əˈtæk /	16
attacker	/ əˈtækə /	16
attend	/ əˈtend /	17
audience	/ ˈɔ:diəns /	13
August	/ ˈɔ:gəst /	9
aunt	/ ɑ:nt /	4
Australia	/ ɒsˈtreɪli:ə /	8
Australian	/ ɒsˈtreɪli:ən /	8
autobiography	/ ɔ:təbaɪˈɒgrəfi: /	13
author	/ ˈɔ:θə /	13
avalanche	/ ˈævəlɑ:nʃ /	8

B		
baby	/ ˈbeɪbi: /	4
back	/ bæk /	7
backache	/ ˈbækeɪk /	7
badly-paid	/ ˈbædli: ˈpeɪd /	2
bag	/ bæg /	17
baggage collection	/ ˈbægɪdʒ kəˈlekʃən /	1
bake	/ beɪk /	5
ball	/ bɔ:l /	6
ballet	/ ˈbæleɪ /	12
bandage	/ ˈbændɪdʒ /	7
Bank Holiday	/ bæŋk ˈhɔlɪdeɪ /	10
bar	/ bɑ: /	12
bargain	/ ˈbɑ:gɪn /	15
barn	/ bɑ:n /	11
basin	/ ˈbeɪsɪn /	3
basketball	/ ˈbɑ:skɪtbɔ:l /	6
bathroom	/ ˈbɑ:θrʊm /	3
baton	/ ˈbætən /	16
beard	/ bɪəd /	4
beat	/ bi:t /	6
bed and breakfast	/ ˈbedənˈbrekfəst /	10
bedroom	/ ˈbedrʊm /	3
beer	/ bɪə /	5
belt	/ belt /	15
bench	/ bentʃ /	11
bicycle	/ ˈbaɪsɪkəl /	1
binoculars	/ bɪˈnɒkjʊləz /	12
biography	/ baɪˈɒgrəfi: /	13
bird	/ bɜ:d /	12
black	/ blæk /	4
blanket	/ blæŋkət /	3
blinds	/ blaɪnz /	3
block of flats	/ blɔkəˈflæts /	11
blouse	/ blaʊz /	15
blow	/ bləʊ /	9
blusher	/ ˈblʌʃə /	15
board	/ bɔ:d /	17
boarding pass	/ ˈbɔ:dɪŋ pɑ:s /	1
boil	/ bɔɪl /	5
boiling	/ ˈbɔɪlɪŋ /	9
bone	/ bəʊn /	7
booked	/ bʊkt /	13
boot	/ bu:t /	15
boring	/ ˈbɔ:rɪŋ /	2
borrow	/ ˈbɒrəʊ /	11
bowl	/ bəʊl /	12
boxer	/ ˈbɒksə /	6
boxing	/ ˈbɒksɪŋ /	6
Boxing Day	/ ˈbɒksɪŋ deɪ /	10
boxing ring	/ ˈbɒksɪŋ rɪŋ /	6
bra	/ brɑ: /	15
bracelet	/ ˈbreɪslət /	15
brain	/ breɪn /	7
brave	/ breɪv /	14
Brazil	/ brəˈzɪl /	8
Brazilian	/ brəˈzɪlɪən /	8
break down	/ breɪk ˈdaʊn /	7
bridge	/ brɪdʒ /	1
briefcase	/ ˈbri:fkeɪs /	15
broken	/ ˈbrəʊkən /	7
brother	/ ˈbrʌðə /	4
brother-in-law	/ ˈbrʌðərɪnlɔ: /	4
brown	/ braʊn /	4
buffet	/ ˈbʌfeɪ /	1
building	/ ˈbɪldɪŋ /	11
building site	/ ˈbɪldɪŋ saɪt /	11
bungalow	/ ˈbʌŋgələʊ /	11
bus	/ bʌs /	1
bus station	/ ˈbʌsteɪʃən /	1
by hand	/ baɪ ˈhænd /	2
bypass	/ ˈbaɪ pɑ:s /	1

C		
cabaret	/ ˈkæbəreɪ /	12
café	/ ˈkæfeɪ /	5
calculator	/ ˈkælkjʊleɪtə /	2
camera	/ ˈkæmərə /	12
camping	/ ˈkæmpɪŋ /	6
campsite	/ ˈkæmpsaɪt /	10
can	/ kæn /	12
Canada	/ ˈkænədə /	8
Canadian	/ kəˈneɪdɪən /	8
canal	/ kəˈnæl /	8
canoeing	/ kəˈnu:ɪŋ /	10
canteen	/ kænˈti:n /	5
cap	/ kæp /	15
capital city	/ ˈkæpɪtəl ˈcɪti: /	8
captain	/ ˈkæptən /	6
car	/ kɑ: /	1
caravan	/ ˈkærəvæn /	1
car hire	/ ˈkɑ: haɪə /	11
car park	/ ˈkɑ: pɑ:k /	10
Caribbean	/ kærɪˈbi:ən /	8
carpentry	/ ˈkɑ:pəntri: /	17
carpet	/ ˈkɑ:pət /	3
cassette	/ kəˈset /	13
catch	/ kætʃ /	6
central	/ ˈsentrəl /	11
ceremony	/ ˈserəməni: /	14
certificate	/ səˈtɪfɪkət /	17
chalet	/ ˈʃæleɪ /	10

chalk / tʃɔ:k / 17
change / tʃeɪndʒ / 10
charge / tʃɑ:dʒ / 16
chase / tʃeɪs / 16
checked / tʃekt / 15
check in / ˈtʃek ɪn / 10
check up / ˈtʃek ʌp / 7
chef / ʃef / 2
chest / tʃest / 7
child / tʃaɪld / 4
childlike / ˈtʃaɪldlaɪk / 4
childish / ˈtʃaɪldɪʃ / 4
chimney / ˈtʃɪmnɪ: / 11
China / ˈtʃaɪnə / 8
Chinese / tʃaɪˈni:z / 8
chiropodist / kɪˈrɒpədɪst / 7
choose / tʃu:z / 15
Christmas Day / ˈkrɪsməs ˈdeɪ / 10
Christmas Eve / ˈkrɪsməs ˈi:v / 10
church spire / tʃ3:tʃ ˈspaɪə / 11
cider / ˈsaɪdə / 5
cinema / sɪnəmɑ: / 12
city / ˈsɪti: / 8
clapping / ˈklæpɪŋ / 13
clean / kli:n / 2
cleaning / ˈkli:nɪŋ / 3
clear / klɪə / 9
climbing / ˈklaɪmɪŋ / 10
cloud / klaʊd / 9
cloudy / ˈklaʊdi: / 9
club / klʌb / 6
clue / klu: / 16
coach / kəʊtʃ / 1
coach station / ˈkəʊtʃ steɪʃən / 1
coastal / ˈkəʊstəl / 11
coat / kəʊt / 15
cold / kəʊld / 9
colleague / ˈkɒli:g / 14
collect / kəˈlekt / 12
collector / kəˈlektə / 12
college / ˈkɒlədʒ / 17
comedy / ˈkɒmədi: / 13
commercial / kəˈm3:ʃəl / 11
commit / kəˈmɪt / 16
compact disc / ˈkɒmpæk ˈdɪsk / 13
comparison / kəmˈpærɪsən / 14
compartment / kəmˈpɑ:tmənt / 1
composer / kəmˈpəʊzə / 13
computer / kəmˈpju:tə / 2
computer studies / kəmˈpju:tə ˈstʌdɪ:z / 17
concert hall / ˈkɒnsət hɔ:l / 12
conductor / kənˈdʌktə / 13
confetti / kənˈfeti: / 14
confident / ˈkɒnfɪdənt / 4
constable / ˈkɒnstəbəl / 16
contract [n] / ˈkɒntrækt / 11
conviction / kənˈvɪkʃən / 16
corner / ˈkɔ:nə / 1
cooked / kʊkt / 5
cooker / ˈkʊkə / 3
cookery / ˈkʊkəri: / 17
cooking / ˈkʊkɪŋ / 3
cool / ku:l / 9
cost / kɒst / 15
cottage / ˈkɒtədʒ / 11
cotton / ˈkɒtən / 15
court of law / kɔ:təvˈlɔ: / 16
courtesy bus / ˈk3:təsi: ˈbʌs / 10
cousin / ˈkʌzɪn / 4
coward / ˈkaʊəd / 14
cricket pitch / ˈkrɪkɪt ˈpɪtʃ / 6
crime / kraɪm / 16
crossing / ˈkrɒsɪŋ / 1
crossroads / ˈkrɒsrəʊdz / 1
cry / krai / 14
Cup / kʌp / 6
cupboard / ˈkʌbəd / 3
curly / ˈk3:li: / 4
curry / ˈkʌri: / 5
curtain / ˈk3:tən / 13
cushion / ˈkʊʃən / 3
Customs / ˈkʌstəms / 1
cut down / kʌt ˈdaʊn / 7
cycling / ˈsaɪklɪŋ / 6
cyclist / ˈsaɪklɪst / 6

D

dance / dɑ:ns / 13
dancer / ˈdɑ:nsə / 13
dangerous / ˈdeɪndʒərəs / 12
dark / dɑ:k / 4
date / deɪt / 14
dawn / dɔ:n / 8
December / dəˈsembə / 9
decent / ˈdi:sənt / 14
decorate / ˈdekəreɪt / 11
degree / dəˈgri: / 17
delayed / dəˈleɪd / 10
dentist / ˈdentɪst / 7
departure lounge / dɪˈpɑ:tʃə laʊndʒ / 1
design / dəˈzaɪn / 12
desk / desk / 2
despised / dəsˈpaɪzd / 14
destination / destɪˈneɪʃən / 10
detective / dəˈtektɪv / 12
diary / ˈdaɪəri: / 2
direct / daɪˈrekt / 1
dining room / ˈdaɪnɪŋ rʊm / 10
director / dɪˈrektə / 13
dirty / ˈd3:ti: / 2
disapprove / dɪsəˈpru:v / 14
disco / ˈdɪskəʊ / 12
dishonest / dɪsˈɒnɪst / 4
dislike / dɪsˈlaɪk / 14
divided / dɪˈvaɪdɪd / 17
dock / dɒk / 16
doctor / ˈdɒktə / 7
doorstep / ˈdɔ:step / 11
documentary / dɒkjʊˈmentəri: / 12
doubles / ˈdʌbəlz / 10
do without / du: wɪˈðaʊt / 7
draught / drɑ:ft / 8
drink driving / drɪŋk ˈdraɪvɪŋ / 16
drive / draɪv / 11
drop / drɒp / 9
drug squad / ˈdrʌgskwɒd / 16
drummer / ˈdrʌmə / 13
drums / drʌmz / 13
dry / draɪ / 9
dusk / dʌsk / 8
dusting / ˈdʌstɪŋ / 3
Dutch / dʌtʃ / 8
duty free / dju:tɪ ˈfri: / 1

E

ear / ɪə / 7
earn / 3:n / 2
earnings / ˈ3:nɪŋs / 2
earrings / ˈɪərɪŋs / 2
earth / 3:θ / 8
earthquake / ˈ3:θkweɪk / 8
east / i:st / 9
Easter / ˈi:stə / 10
easy / ˈi:si: / 2
economics / ekəˈnɒmɪks / 17
education / edʒʊˈkeɪʃən / 17
elbow / ˈelbəʊ / 7
elderly / ˈeldə:li: / 4
embarrassed / ɪmˈbærəsd / 14
emergency / ɪˈm3:dʒənsi: / 3
employ / ɪmˈplɔɪ / 2
employment / ɪmˈplɔɪmənt / 2
enclose / enˈkləʊz / 2

enemy	/ ˈenəmi: /	14
energetic	/ enɜ:ˈdʒetɪk /	12
engagement	/ enˈgeɪdʒmənt /	14
England	/ ˈɪŋglənd /	8
English	/ ˈɪŋglɪʃ /	8
enthusiastic	/ ɪnθju:zi:ˈæstɪk /	4
envious	/ ˈenvi:əs /	14
envy	/ ˈenvi: /	14
equals	/ ˈi:kwəlz /	17
equator	/ ɪˈkweɪtə /	8
estate agent	/ ɪˈsteɪt eɪdʒənt /	11
exciting	/ ɪkˈsaɪtɪŋ /	12
excursion	/ ɪksˈkɜ:ʃən /	10
exercise	/ ˈeksɜ:saɪz /	6
exercise book	/ ˈeksɜ:saɪz bʊk /	17
exit	/ ˈeksɪt /	1
extension	/ eksˈtenʃən /	11
eyes	/ aɪz /	7
eye shadow	/ ˈaɪ ʃædəʊ /	15
F		
facilities	/ fəˈsɪlɪti:z /	10
fail	/ feɪl /	17
fair	/ feə /	4
fairy story	/ ˈfeəri: ˈstɔ:ri: /	13
fall [v]	/ fɔ:l /	9
famous	/ ˈfeɪməs /	13
farmhouse	/ ˈfɑ:mhaʊs /	11
Farsi	/ ˈfɑ:si: /	8
favourite	/ ˈfeɪvərɪt /	12
fear	/ fɪə /	14
February	/ ˈfebrʊəri: /	9
fence	/ fens /	11
ferry	/ ˈferi: /	1
ferry port	/ ˈferi: pɔ:t /	1
field	/ fi:ld /	11
filing cabinet	/ ˈfaɪlɪŋ ˈkæbɪnət /	2
fill	/ fɪl /	5
film	/ fɪlm /	12
financial	/ fɪˈnænʃəl /	11
fine	/ faɪn /	16
finger	/ ˈfɪŋgə /	7
first class	/ fɜ:st ˈklɑ:s /	1
fit [adj]	/ fɪt /	12
fit [v]	/ fit/	15
flannel	/ ˈflænəl /	3
flight	/ flaɪt /	10
flood	/ flʌd /	8
floral	/ ˈflɔ:rəl /	15
food poisoning	/ ˈfu:d ˈpɔɪsənɪŋ /	10
fog	/ fɒg /	9
foggy	/ ˈfɒgi: /	9
foolish	/ ˈfu:lɪʃ /	14
foot	/ fʊt /	10
football	/ ˈfʊtbɔ:l /	6
foreigner	/ ˈfɒrənə /	10
foreign language	/ ˈfɒrən ˈlæŋgwɪdʒ /	17
forest	/ ˈfɒrɪst /	8
forest fire	/ ˈfɒrɪst ˈfaɪə /	8
France	/ frɑ:ns /	8
freeze	/ frɪ:z /	9
freezer	/ fri:zə /	3
freezing	/ ˈfri:zɪŋ /	9
French	/ frentʃ /	8
fresh	/ freʃ /	5
friend	/ frend /	14
friendly	/ ˈfrendli: /	4
fridge	/ frɪdʒ /	3
front door	/ frʌnt ˈdɔ: /	11
front garden	/ frʌnt ˈgɑ:dən /	11
frost	/ frɒst /	9
frosty	/ ˈfrɒsti: /	9
fry	/ fraɪ /	5
frying pan	/ ˈfraɪɪŋ pæn /	5
full-time	/ fʊl ˈtaɪm /	2
furnish	/ ˈfɜ:nɪʃ /	11
further education	/ ˈfɜ:ðə edjʊˈkeɪʃən /	17
G		
gale	/ geɪl /	9
games room	/ ˈgeɪmz rʊm /	3
gang	/ gæŋ /	16
garage	/ ˈgærɪdʒ /	11
garden pond	/ ˈgɑ:dən ˈpɒnd /	11
garden shed	/ ˈgɑ:dən ˈʃed /	11
gardener	/ ˈgɑ:dənə /	12
gardening	/ ˈgɑ:dənɪŋ /	12
gate	/ geɪt /	11
geography	/ dʒi:ˈɒgrəfi: /	17
German	/ ˈdʒɜ:mən /	8
Germany	/ ˈdʒɜ:məni: /	8
ginger	/ ˈdʒɪndʒə /	4
give up	/ gɪv ʌp /	7
glasses	/ ˈglɑ:sɪs /	15
glove	/ glʌv /	6
goal	/ gəʊl /	6
golf	/ gɒlf /	6
gold	/ gəʊld /	15
Good Friday	/ gʊd ˈfraɪdeɪ /	10
grandparents	/ ˈgrænpeərənts /	4
grateful	/ ˈgreɪtfəl /	2
Greece	/ gri:s /	8
greed	/ gri:d /	14
greedy	/ ˈgri:di: /	14
grill	/ grɪl /	5
guest	/ gest /	10
guesthouse	/ ˈgesthaʊs /	10
guide	/ gaɪd /	10
guilty	/ ˈgɪlti: /	16
guitar	/ gɪˈtɑ: /	13
guitarist	/ gɪˈtɑ:rɪst /	13
gym	/ dʒɪm /	3
gymnast	/ ˈdʒɪmnæst /	6
gymnastics	/ dʒɪmˈnæstɪks /	6
H		
hair	/ heə /	4
hall	/ hɔ:l /	3
hamburger	/ ˈhæmbɜ:gə /	5
hand	/ hænd /	7
handbag	/ ˈhændbæg /	15
handcuffs	/ ˈhændkʌfs /	16
handkerchief	/ ˈhæŋkətʃɪf /	15
hang gliding	/ ˈhæŋ glaɪdɪŋ /	12
hat	/ hæt /	15
hate	/ heɪt /	14
haystack	/ ˈheɪstæk /	11
head	/ hed /	7
headache	/ ˈhedeɪk /	7
headphones	/ ˈhedfəʊnz /	13
heart	/ hɑ:t /	7
heavy	/ ˈhevi: /	9
hedge	/ hedʒ /	11
helmet	/ ˈhelmət /	16
hemisphere	/ ˈhemɪsfi:ə /	8
herbs	/ hɜ:bz /	12
hero	/ ˈhɪərəʊ /	14
high	/ haɪ /	9
hill	/ hɪl /	8
historic	/ hɪsˈtɒrɪk /	10
history	/ ˈhɪstəri: /	17
hi-fi	/ ˈhaɪfaɪ /	13
hi-jack	/ ˈhaɪdʒæk /	16
hi-jacker	/ ˈhaɪdʒækə /	16
hit	/ hɪt /	6
holiday representative	/ ˈhɒlɪdeɪ reprɪˈsentətɪv /	10
Holland	/ ˈhɒlənd /	8
honest	/ ˈɒnɪst /	4
honeymoon	/ ˈhʌni:mu:n /	14
hooped	/ hu:pt /	15
hoovering	/ ˈhu:vərɪŋ /	3
horror	/ ˈhɒrə /	13
horse-rider	/ ˈhɔ:s raɪdə /	6

horse-riding / ˈhɔ:s raɪdɪŋ / 6
hot / hɒt / 9
hotplate / ˈhɒtpleɪt / 5
hotel / həʊˈtel / 10
houseboat / ˈhaʊsbəʊt / 11
housework / ˈhaʊswɜ:k / 3
housing estate / ˈhaʊzɪŋ esˈteɪt / 11
hovercraft / ˈhɒvəkrɑ:ft / 1
humidity / hju:ˈmɪdɪti: / 9
hurricane / ˈhʌrɪkən / 8
hurt / hɜ:t / 7
husband / ˈhʌzbənd / 3

I

ice-skater / ˈaɪskeɪtə / 6
ice-skating / ˈaɪskeɪtɪŋ / 6
icy / ˈaɪsi: / 7
identify / aɪˈdentɪfaɪ / 16
illegally / ɪˈli:gəlɪ: / 16
immature / ɪməˈtʃuə / 4
immigration / ɪmɪˈgreɪʃən / 1
impatient / ɪmˈpeɪʃənt / 4
India / ˈɪndi:ə / 8
Indian / ˈɪndi:ən / 8
inexpensive / ɪneksˈpensɪv / 12
initials / ɪˈnɪʃəlz / 2
injection / ɪnˈdʒekʃən / 7
innocent / ˈɪnəsənt / 16
inspector / ɪnˈspektə / 1
instrument / ˈɪnstrəmənt / 13
insult [n] / ˈɪnsʌlt / 14
intelligence / ɪnˈtelɪdʒəns / 17
interesting / ˈɪntrəstɪŋ / 2
interval / ˈɪntəvəl / 13
interview / ˈɪntəvju: / 16
Iran / ɪˈrɑ:n / 8
Iranian / ɪˈreɪni:ən / 8
Irish / ˈaɪərɪʃ / 8
ironing / ˈaɪənɪŋ / 3

J

jacket / ˈdʒækət / 15
January / ˈdʒænjuəri: / 9
Japan / dʒəˈpæn / 8
Japanese / dʒæpəˈni:z / 8
jealous / ˈdʒeləs / 14
jeans / dʒi:nz / 15
jogging / ˈdʒɒgɪŋ / 6
journey / ˈdʒɜ:ni: / 1
judge / dʒʌdʒ / 16
jumper / ˈdʒʌmpə / 15
June / dʒu:n / 9
July / dʒu:ˈlaɪ / 9
jury / ˈdʒʊəri: / 16

K

Kenya / ˈkenjə / 8
kerb / kɜ:b / 11
kettle / ˈketl / 5
keys / ki:z / 11
kick / kɪk / 6
kind / kaɪnd / 4
kit / kɪt / 6
kitchen / ˈkɪtʃɪn / 3
knee / ni: / 7
knickers / ˈnɪkəz / 15
knowledge / ˈnɒlədʒ / 17

L

lake / leɪk / 8
lamp post / ˈlæmp pəʊst / 11
landing / ˈlændɪŋ / 3
landlady / ˈlændleɪdi: / 11
landlord / ˈlændlɔ:d / 11
lane / leɪn / 11
language / ˈlæŋgwɪdʒ / 13
lawyer / ˈlɔɪjə / 16
learn / lɜ:n / 12
learning / ˈlɜ:nɪŋ / 17
leather / ˈleðə / 15
leg / leg / 7
liar / ˈlaɪə / 14
light / laɪt / 9
lightning / ˈlaɪtnɪŋ / 9
line / laɪn / 13
liquidiser / ˈlɪkwɪdaɪzə / 5
listener / ˈlɪsnə / 12
lipstick / ˈlɪpstɪk / 15
litter bin / ˈlɪtə bɪn / 11
living room / ˈlɪvɪŋ rʊm / 3
loan / ləʊn / 11
lodger / ˈlɒdʒə / 11
long / lɒŋ / 4
look after / lʊk ˈɑ:ftə / 7
lookout / ˈlʊkaʊt / 16
lose / lu:z / 6
loudspeaker / laʊdˈspi:kə / 13
love story / ˈlʌv stɔ:rɪ: / 13
luggage / ˈlʌgɪdʒ / 10
lung / lʌŋ / 7

M

maintenance / ˈmeɪntənəns / 12
Malta / ˈmɔ:ltə / 8
March / mɑ:tʃ / 9
market place / ˈmɑ:kɪt pleɪs / 11
marriage certificate / ˈmærɪdʒ səˈtɪfɪkət / 14
mascara / mæsˈkɑ:rə / 15
match / mætʃ / 6
maths / mæθs / 17
mature / məˈtʃuə / 4
May / meɪ / 9
May Day / ˈmeɪ deɪ / 10
measure / ˈmeʒə / 15
mechanic / məˈkænɪk / 2
medal / ˈmedəl / 6
melt / melt / 9
mess / mes / 3
Mexican / ˈmeksɪkən / 8
Mexico / ˈmeksɪkəʊ / 8
microwave / ˈmaɪkrəweɪv / 5
midday / mɪˈdeɪ / 8
middle-aged / ˈmɪdl eɪdʒd / 4
midnight / ˈmɪdnaɪt / 8
mild / maɪld / 5
minus / ˈmaɪnəs / 17
mist / mɪst / 9
misty / ˈmɪsti: / 9
mixing / ˈmɪksɪŋ / 12
moon / mu:n / 8
mortgage / ˈmɔ:gɪdʒ / 11
motel / məʊˈtel / 10
mother / ˈmʌðə / 4
motorway / ˈməʊtəweɪ / 1
mountain / ˈmaʊntən / 8
moustache / məsˈtɑ:ʃ / 4
mouth / maʊθ / 7
move in / mu:v ˈɪn / 11
murder / ˈmɜ:də / 16
murderer / ˈmɜ:dərə / 16
musician / mju:ˈzɪʃən / 13

N

napkin / ˈnæpkɪn / 3
neat / ni:t / 5
neck / nek / 7
necklace / ˈnekləs / 15
needle / ˈni:dəl / 13
nephew / ˈnefju: / 4
nervous / ˈnɜ:vəs / 14
net / net / 6
news / nju:z / 12
New Year's Day / nju: jɪəz ˈdeɪ / 10
New Year's Eve / nju: jɪəz ˈi:v / 10
New Zealand / nju: ˈzi:lənd / 8

niece / ni:s / 4
Nigeria / naɪˈdʒɪərɪə / 8
nightclub / ˈnaɪtklʌb / 12
Northern **Ire**land / ˈnɔ:ðən ˈaɪələnd / 8
nose / nəʊz / 7
no **smok**ing com**part**ment / nəʊ ˈsməʊkɪŋ kəmˈpɑ:tmənt / 1
notebook / ˈnəʊtbʊk / 16
note pad / ˈnəʊtpæd / 2
novel / ˈnɒvəl / 13
No**vem**ber / nəʊˈvembə / 9
nurse / nɜ:s / 2
nylon / ˈnaɪlɒn / 15

O

ocean / ˈəʊʃən / 8
Oc**to**ber / ɒkˈtəʊbə / 9
off **du**ty / ɒf ˈdju:ti: / 2
of**fence** / əˈfens / 16
offer / ˈɒfə / 2
oil / ɔɪl / 12
ointment / ˈɔɪntmənt / 7
old / əʊld / 4
O**lym**pics / əˈlɪmpɪks / 6
on **du**ty / ɒn ˈdju:ti: / 2
one way **street** / wʌn weɪ ˈstrɪ:t / 1
on **strike** / ɒn ˈstraɪk / 10
op**po**nent / əˈpəʊnənt / 14
op**ti**cian / ɒpˈtɪʃən / 7
orchestra / ˈɔ:kestrə / 13
organ / ˈɔ:gən / 13
out of **or**der / aʊt əv ˈɔ:də / 2
out of **work** / aʊt əv ˈwɜ:k / 2
oven / ʌvən / 5
overcast / ˈəʊvəkɑ:st / 9
own / əʊn / 11

P

package **hol**iday / ˈpækədʒ ˈhɒlɪdeɪ / 10
packet / ˈpækət / 12
paint / peɪnt / 11
palm / pɑ:m / 7
parachuting / ˈpærəʃu:tɪŋ / 12
parking / ˈpɑ:kɪŋ / 16
pa**role** / pəˈrəʊl / 16
part-time / ˈpɑ:taɪm / 2
pass / pɑ:s / 17
pass **out** / pɑ:s ˈaʊt / 7
passport con**trol** / ˈpɑ:spɔ:t kənˈtrəʊl / 1
pasta / ˈpæstə / 5
patient [adj] / ˈpeɪʃənt / 4
patient [n] / ˈpeɪʃənt / 7
path / pɑ:θ / 11
patterned / ˈpætənd / 15
pavement / ˈpeɪvmənt / 11
pay **for** / peɪ ˈfɔ: / 15
pen / pen / 17
pencil / ˈpensɪl / 17
pensioner / ˈpenʃənə / 4
per **cent** / pəˈsent / 17
percolator / ˈpɜ:kəleɪtə / 5
per**form** / pəˈfɔ:m / 13
per**form**ance / pəˈfɔ:məns / 13
permanent / ˈpɜ:mənənt / 2
Pe**ru** / pəˈru: / 8
Pe**ru**vian / pəˈru:vi:ən / 8
photocopier / ˈfəʊtəkɒpɪə / 2
photograph / ˈfəʊtəgrɑ:f / 12
pho**tog**raphy / fəˈtɒgrəfi: / 12
physical edu**ca**tion / ˈfɪzɪkəl edʒʊˈkeɪʃən / 17
pi**an**o / pi:ˈænəʊ / 13
pick **up** / pɪk ˈup / 10
picture / ˈpɪktʃə / 12
pilot / ˈpaɪlət / 2
pillow / ˈpɪləʊ / 3
plain / pleɪn / 15
plane / pleɪn / 1
planet / ˈplænət / 8
platform / ˈplætfɔ:m / 1
play / pleɪ / 13
player / ˈpleɪjə / 6
playschool / ˈpleɪsku:l / 17
pleased / pli:zd / 14
pleasure / ˈpleʒə / 14
plus / plʌs / 17
poetry / ˈpəʊətri: / 13
Pole / pəʊl / 8
polishing / ˈpɒlɪʃɪŋ / 3
po**lite** / pəˈlaɪt / 14
polka-dot / ˈpɒlkə dɒt / 15
poly**tech**nic / pɒlɪˈteknɪk / 17
pony-**trek**king / ˈpəʊni: ˈtrekɪŋ / 10
popular / ˈpɒpjʊlə / 12
porter / ˈpɔ:tə / 10
portrait / ˈpɔ:treɪt / 14
Portugal / ˈpɔ:tʃʊgəl / 8
Portu**guese** / pɔ:tʃʊˈgi:z / 8
po**si**tion / pəˈzɪʃən / 2
pour / pɔ: / 5
pre**scrip**tion / prɪˈskrɪpʃən / 7
price / praɪs / 15
primary / ˈpraɪməri: / 17
principal / ˈprɪnsɪpəl / 17
private / ˈpraɪvət / 17
pro**duc**er / prəˈdju:sə / 13
programme / ˈprəʊgræm / 13
pro**mote** / prəˈməʊt / 2
pro**mo**tion / prəˈməʊʃən / 2
psy**chi**atrist / saɪˈkaɪətrɪst / 7
pull **down** / pʊl ˈdaʊn / 11
purse / pɜ:s / 15

Q

queue / kju: / 13
quiz show / ˈkwɪz ʃəʊ / 12

R

race / reɪs / 6
race-course / ˈreɪs kɔ:s / 6
racing-**dri**ver / ˈreɪsɪŋ ˈdraɪvə / 6
racing-**dri**ving / ˈreɪsɪŋ ˈdraɪvɪŋ / 6
racket / ˈrækət / 6
radio / ˈreɪdɪəʊ / 16
rain / reɪn / 9
rainy / ˈreɪni: / 9
raw / rɔ: / 5
re**cep**tion / rəˈsepʃən / 10
recipe / ˈresɪpi: / 12
record [n] / ˈrekɔ:d / 6
record **play**er / ˈrekɔ:d ˈpleɪjə / 13
red / red / 4
registry **of**fice / ˈredʒɪstri: ˈɒfɪs / 14
re**lax**ing / rɪˈlæksɪŋ / 12
re**lease** / rɪˈli:s / 16
re**li**able / rɪˈlaɪəbəl / 4
renting / ˈrentɪŋ / 11
Re**pub**lic of **Ire**land / rɪˈpʌblɪk əv ˈaɪələnd / 8
re**serve** / rɪˈzɜ:v / 1
resi**den**tial / rezɪˈdenʃəl / 11
restaurant / ˈrestərɒnt / 5
retake / ˈri:teɪk / 17
re**tire** / rɪˈtaɪə / 2
re**tire**ment / rɪˈtaɪəmənt / 2
re**turn** / rɪˈtɜ:n / 1
ride / raɪd / 1
ring / rɪŋ / 14
ring **up** / rɪŋ ˈʌp / 10
riot shield / ˈraɪət ʃi:ld / 16
ripe / raɪp / 5
rise / raɪz / 9

river / ˈrɪvə / 8
roast / rəʊst / 5
rob / rɒb / 16
robber / ˈrɒbə / 16
role / rəʊl / 13
romantic / rəˈmæntɪk / 13
room / rʊm / 11
room service / ˈrʊm sɜːvɪs / 10
root / ruːt / 11
rough / rʌf / 9
roundabout / ˈraʊndəbaʊt / 1
row of seats / rəʊ əv ˈsiːts / 13
rubber / ˈrʌbə / 17
rug / rʌg / 3
rugby / ˈrʌgbiː / 6
ruler / ˈruːlə / 17
runner / ˈrʌnə / 6
running / ˈrʌnɪŋ / 6

S

sad / sæd / 14
sadness / ˈsædnɪs / 14
sailing / ˈseɪlɪŋ / 10
sales assistant / ˈseɪlz əˈsɪstənt / 2
saucepan / ˈsɔːspən / 5
Saudi Arabia / ˈsaʊdiː əˈreɪbiːə / 8
Saudi Arabian / ˈsaʊdiː əˈreɪbiːən /8
saxophone / ˈsæksəfəʊn / 13
saxophonist / sæˈksɒfənɪst / 13
scarf / skɑːf / 15
scenery / ˈsiːnəriː / 10
science / ˈsaɪəns / 17
Scotland / ˈskɒtlənd / 8
Scottish / ˈskɒtɪʃ / 8
screen / skriːn / 13
sea / siː / 10
search for / sɜːtʃ ˈfɔː / 16
seat number / ˈsiːt nʌmbə / 1
secondary / ˈsekəndriː / 17
second-hand / sekənd ˈhænd / 15
seed / siːd / 12
selfish / ˈselfɪʃ / 14
semi-detached / semiː dəˈtætʃd / 11
sensible / ˈsensɪbəl / 14
sensitive / ˈsensɪtɪv / 14
sentence / ˈsentəns / 16
September / sepˈtembə / 9
sew / səʊ / 12
sewing / ˈsəʊwɪŋ / 17
sheet / ʃiːt / 3
shine / ʃaɪn / 9
shirt / ʃɜːt / 15
shoe / ʃuː / 12
shoplift / ˈʃɒplɪft / 16
shoplifter / ˈʃɒplɪftə / 16
shopping / ˈʃɒpɪŋ / 3
short / ʃɔːt / 4
shorten / ˈʃɔːtən / 15
shorts / ʃɔːts / 15
shoulder / ˈʃəʊldə / 7
shout / ʃaʊt / 14
shower / ˈʃaʊə / 9
shutter / ˈʃʌtə / 11
side / saɪd / 6
sightseeing / ˈsaɪtsiːɪŋ / 10
signature / ˈsɪgnətʃə / 2
silk / sɪlk / 15
silver / ˈsɪlvə / 15
single / ˈsɪŋgəl / 1
sink / sɪŋk / 3
sip / sɪp / 5
site / saɪt / 10
size / saɪz / 15
skiing / ˈskiːɪŋ / 6
skilled / skɪld / 2
skirt / skɜːt / 15
sky / skaɪ / 9
smuggle / ˈsmʌgəl / 16
smuggler / ˈsmʌglə / 16
snooker / ˈsnuːkə / 6
snow / snəʊ / 9
snowfall / ˈsnəʊfɔːl / 9
snowy / ˈsnəʊwiː / 9
soap opera / səʊp ˈɒpərə / 12
sociable / ˈsəʊʃəbəl / 12
sock / sɒk / 15
sofa / ˈsəʊfə / 3
solicitor / səˈlɪsɪtə / 16
sour / saʊə / 5
south / saʊθ / 9
souvenir / suːvəˈniːə / 10
spade / speɪd / 12
Spanish / ˈspænɪʃ / 8
spanner / ˈspænə / 12
spare room / speə ˈrʊm / 3
spectator / spekˈteɪtə / 6
speech / spiːtʃ / 14
speeding / ˈspiːdɪŋ / 16
spicy / ˈspaɪsiː / 5
sport / spɔːt / 6
spring / sprɪŋ / 9
squared / skweərd / 17
square root / skweə ˈruːt / 17
squash / skwɒʃ / 6
stage / steɪdʒ / 13
stairs / steəz / 3
stale / steɪl / 5
stamp / stæmp / 12
stand / stænd / 5
standard class / ˈstændəd klɑːs / 1
star / stɑː / 13
state / steɪt / 17
steal / stiːl / 16
steam / stiːm / 5
steward / ˈstjuːəd / 2
stewardess / stjuːəˈdɪs / 2
stick / stɪk / 15
stir / stɜː / 5
stir-fry / ˈstɜː fraɪ / 5
stolen / ˈstəʊlən / 10
stomach / ˈstʌmək / 7
stomach ache / ˈstʌməkeɪk / 7
storm / stɔːm / 9
story / ˈstɔːriː / 12
straight / streɪt / 4
stranger / ˈstreɪndʒə / 10
straw / strɔː / 15
stream / striːm / 11
stressful / ˈstresfəl / 2
striped / straɪpt / 15
strong / strɒŋ / 9
study / ˈstʌdiː / 17
suburban / səˈbɜːbən / 11
subway / ˈsʌbweɪ / 1
suit / suːt / 15
suitcase / ˈsuːtkeɪs / 10
summer / ˈsʌmə / 9
sun / sʌn / 8
sunbathing / ˈsʌnbeɪðɪŋ / 10
sunny period / ˈsʌniː ˈpɪərɪəd / 9
sunny spell / ˈsʌniː spel / 9
sunstroke / ˈsʌnstrəʊk / 10
surfing / ˈsɜːfɪŋ / 6
surgeon / ˈsɜːdʒən / 7
surname / ˈsɜːneɪm / 2
survey [n] / ˈsɜːveɪ / 11
suspect [n] / ˈsʌspekt / 16
suspect [v] / səsˈpekt / 16
sweet / swiːt / 5
swimming pool / ˈswɪmɪŋ puːl / 6
swimsuit / ˈswɪmsuːt / 6

T

tablecloth / ˈteɪbəlklɒθ / 3
tablet / ˈtæblət / 7
take an exam / teɪk ən ɪgˈzæm / 17

takeaway / ˈteɪkəweɪ / 5
take **off** / teɪk ˈɒf / 15
take **up** / teɪk ˈʌp / 12
tartan / ˈtɑ:tən / 15
taxi / ˈtæksi: / 1
taxi rank / ˈtæksi: ræŋk / 1
team / ti:m / 6
tech**nical drawing** / ˈteknɪkəl ˈdrɔ:ɪŋ / 17
teenager / ˈti:neɪdʒə / 4
tele**phone** direc**tory** / ˈteləfəʊn dəˈrektəri: / 2
temperature / ˈtempərətʃə / 7
temporary / ˈtempərəri: / 2
tenant / ˈtenənt / 11
tender / ˈtendə / 5
tennis / ˈtenɪs / 6
tennis court / ˈtenɪs kɔ:t / 6
tent / tent / 10
terraced / ˈterəsd / 11
textbook / ˈtekstbʊk / 13
theatre / ˈθɪətə / 12
ther**mometer** / θəˈmɒmətə / 5
thick / θɪk / 4
thin / θɪn / 4
thigh / θaɪ / 7
thriller / ˈθrɪlə / 13
throw / θrəʊ / 6
thunder / ˈθʌndə / 9
ticket office / ˈtɪkət ˈɒfɪs / 1
tidying / ˈtaɪdi:ɪŋ / 3
tie / taɪ / 15
timetable / ˈtaɪmteɪbəl / 17
tipping / ˈtɪpɪŋ / 10
T-junction / ˈti:dʒʌŋkʃən / 1
toaster / ˈtəʊstə / 5
toddler / ˈtɒdlə / 4
toe / təʊ / 7
tool / tu:l / 12
tooth / tu:θ / 7
toothache / ˈtu:θeɪk / 7
tough / tʌf / 5
tour / tʊə / 10
tourist / ˈtʊərɪst / 10
tourist inform**ation** office / ˈtʊərɪst ɪnfəˈmeɪʃən ˈɒfɪs / 1
tour leader / ˈtʊə ˈli:də / 10
towel / ˈtaʊəl / 3
town / taʊn / 8
track / træk / 11
tracksuit / ˈtræksu:t / 12
tractor / ˈtræktə / 11

traffic lights / ˈtræfɪk laɪts / 1
traffic warden / ˈtræfɪk ˈwɔ:dən / 16
trail / treɪl / 11
train [n] / treɪn / 1
train [v] / treɪn / 6
trainers / ˈtreɪnəz / 15
travel agent / ˈtrævəl ˈeɪdʒənt / 10
traveller's cheque / ˈtrævələs tʃek / 10
trial / ˈtraɪəl / 16
trip / trɪp / 10
trolley / ˈtrɒli: / 1
trousers / ˈtraʊzəz / 15
trumpet / ˈtrʌmpət / 13
trumpeter / ˈtrʌmpətə / 13
truncheon / ˈtrʌnʃən / 16
try **on** / traɪ ˈɒn / 15
tube / tju:b / 1
tunnel /tʌnəl / 1
Turkey / ˈtɜ:ki: / 8
Turkish / ˈtɜ:kɪʃ / 8
typewriter / ˈtaɪpraɪtə / 2
typing / ˈtaɪpɪŋ / 17

U
um**brella** / ʌmˈbrelə / 15
uncle / ˈʌŋkəl / 4
un**confident** / ʌnˈcɒnfɪdənt / 4
Underground / ˈʌndəgraʊnd / 1
underpants / ˈʌndəpænts / 15
uniform / ˈju:nɪfɔ:m / 16
United States of America / ju:ˈnaɪtəd steɪts əv əmerɪkə / 8
university / ju:nɪˈvɜ:sɪti: / 17
un**kind** / ʌnˈkaɪnd / 4
un**pack** / ʌnˈpæk / 10
unreliable / ʌnrɪˈlaɪəbəl / 4
un**ripe** / ʌnˈraɪp / 5
un**selfish** / ʌnˈselfɪʃ / 4
un**skilled** / ʌnˈskɪld / 2
upbringing / ˈʌpbrɪŋɪŋ / 17
up to **date** / ʌp tə ˈdeɪt / 2

V
vacci**nation** / væksɪˈneɪʃən / 7
value / ˈvælju: / 15
VDU screen / vi:di:ˈju: skri:n / 2
vegetable / ˈvedʒtəbəl / 12
verdict / ˈvɜ:dɪkt / 16
vest / vest / 15
village pond / ˈvɪlɪdʒ pɒnd / 11
vio**lin** / vaɪəˈlɪn / 13

violinist / vaɪəˈlɪnɪst / 13
visitor / ˈvɪsɪtə / 10
visor / ˈvaɪzə / 16
vodka / ˈvɒdkə / 5
vol**cano** / vɒlˈkeɪnəʊ / 8
voluntary / ˈvɒləntri: / 12

W
waiter / ˈweɪtə / 2
waitress / ˈweɪtrɪs / 2
wallet / ˈwɒlət / 15
washing / ˈwɒʃɪŋ / 3
washing ma**chine** / ˈwɒʃɪŋ məˈʃi:n / 3
washing up / ˈwɒʃɪŋ ˈʌp / 3
watch / wɒtʃ / 12
watcher / ˈwɒtʃə / 12
wavy / ˈweɪvi: / 4
wedding / ˈwedɪŋ / 14
weep / wi:p / 14
well-**paid** / wel ˈpeɪd / 2
Welsh / welʃ / 8
west / west / 9
West **Indian** / west ˈɪndi:ən / 8
whistle / ˈwɪsəl / 6
win / wɪn / 6
wind / wɪnd / 9
window sill / ˈwɪndəʊ sɪl / 1
windsurfing / ˈwɪndsɜ:fɪŋ / 6
windy / ˈwɪndi: / 9
wine / waɪn / 5
winter / ˈwɪntə / 9
wipe your **tears** / ˈwaɪp jɔ: ˈtɪəz / 14
witness / ˈwɪtnɪs / 16
witness box / ˈwɪtnɪs bɒks / 16
whirlpool / ˈwɜ:lpu:l / 8
whisky / ˈwɪski: / 5
white / waɪt / 5
wood / wʊd / 8
wool / wʊl / 15
worried / ˈwʌrɪd / 14
worth / wɜ:θ / 15
wrist / rɪst / 7
write / raɪt / 13

Y
youthful / ˈju:θfəl / 4

Z
Zim**bab**we / zɪmˈbɑ:bwi: / 8